SKILFUL RUGBY

SKILFUL RUGBY

RAY WILLIAMS

Welsh Rugby Union
Coaching Organiser

SOUVENIR PRESS

First published 1976 by Souvenir Press Ltd,
43 Great Russell Street, London WC1B 3PA
and simultaneously in Canada by
Methuen Publications,
Agincourt, Ontario

ISBN 0 285 62233 1

Filmset in Photon Times 12 on 14 pt by
Richard Clay (The Chaucer Press), Ltd, Bungay, Suffolk
and printed in Great Britain by
Fletcher & Son Ltd, Norwich

CONTENTS

To

Rugby men the world over, from whom I have learnt so much.

AUTHOR'S NOTE

I hope this book will appeal to player, coach or indeed anyone who is interested in Rugby Football. I have tried in it to reflect the dramatic changes which have taken place over the past ten years. It is a follow-up to my previous book *Rugby for Beginners* and therefore I do not deal at all with individual techniques. I have attempted, in particular, to outline the principles of Rugby Football both in coaching and playing. I feel these to be infinitely more important than some of the intricate detail which in the final analysis has little effect on the way we play the game.

I must thank John Dawes for agreeing to write the Foreword. His contribution to the game as player, captain and coach has been of untold value. He has set standards which are targets for everyone.

I am deeply indebted to E. Gwyn Evans, Lecturer in Physical Education, University College of Wales, Aberystwyth, and a WRU Staff Coach, for the immense help he has given me in writing up the material on fitness. I have worked with him for many years and his lively mind has produced many original ideas which have been incorporated in our coaching methods.

I am grateful to John Pottinger for so ably producing the line drawings, to Mrs Carole Tucker who typed the script and to the many players, wittingly or otherwise, who acted as demonstrators for the photographs for which, as photographer, only I can accept responsibility.

FOREWORD

When Ray Williams told me that he was writing a second book on Rugby football I, probably like all those who know him and certainly those who read his first book, looked forward to the publication with eager anticipation. To be asked to write a foreword was a great thrill and an invitation I readily accepted, if only to attempt to repay all the help he has given me as a player, a captain and, more recently, in the field of coaching.

For me it was somewhat of a surprise when Ray wrote one book, let alone two, because the whole essence of his profession as Coaching Organiser to the WRU he interprets as a practical one, and therefore to find the time must have been difficult indeed. I make the point because in writing this book he has transferred his "practical attitude" into print. Far too many authors in writing about Rugby football end up with a theoretical text which in many instances bears little resemblance to the practical aspects of the modern game.

Although there have been significant changes in the Laws of the game there is little doubt that the largest contributory factor affecting the game has been the coaching and the organisation thereof. That Ray Williams has been a major influence in this department there can be no doubt, but how interesting it is to read in the opening section of the book about the problems that existed in Rugby football's organisation and how Ray managed, through perseverance in most cases, and dedication in all, to overcome them. The quality of play that now exists, certainly in Wales, has come about largely as a result of his efforts and must give him great personal satisfaction.

However, the most pleasing aspect of the book is that it is about Rugby football *AS IT IS NOW*. As indicated above, many Rugby books are concerned with what their respective authors think the game *ought* to be without really understanding modern developments and necessary techniques. Ray in his own inimitable and forceful way has produced a book which will not only be interesting to everyone associated with Rugby football, but will undoubtedly be of enormous help to administrators and coaches and to those who matter most—the players! What has made it even more forceful is that it is backed by comments from senior players who are involved with Rugby football at the highest level. What better conditions could you have for writing a textbook, than a class of demonstrators who are a National XV performing in their games what you write.

The sections on the basic techniques of the game are a must for all players and coaches, whether they are back- or forward-orientated, because as Ray so correctly points out—"once possession is won, the game is about fifteen players". But in all sections, and this is one of the essential features of the book, while realising the essential "*musts*" in technique there is also scope for the individual player both as a thinking and as a practical man. In no way can this book be responsible for turning out "factory-produced players" —which has been one of the criticisms laid at the door of coaching.

Having dealt so well with the basics of the game, the units within a team and their respective roles, Ray has wisely dealt with how the individual can achieve these ideals in what is now a very demanding game. *All* players who seek no more than enjoyment from the game, but especially those who have set their sights on the coveted "cap", would be wise to take heed of what is written, and perhaps more important, implement it.

In conclusion I would say that it has given me great pleasure to write this foreword but even greater pleasure to read the text. If I could be allowed to add a further comment it would be that this book epitomises all that I feel about Rugby football. It can be summed up in a single phrase—"ENJOYMENT VIA QUALITY".

22nd June 1976   JOHN DAWES OBE

SECTION I
Philosophy, Structure and Organisation

1 HISTORICAL BACKGROUND

The decade which bridged the nineteen-sixties and seventies saw in British Rugby Union Football the most remarkable development ever seen in the history of the game. I doubt, in fact, whether any other sport could match such a transformation at any time. This period heralded a dramatic change in attitudes which was reflected in the preparation of international teams, the alteration in laws, the establishment of national competitions and replacements for injured players, to name but a few.

However, the most emotive Rugby term of the era was without doubt the word "coaching". For years in the British Isles there had been a marked reluctance on the part of the governing bodies of Rugby Union Football to develop any scheme aimed at the coaching and preparation of senior players. Events have subsequently proved that this attitude kept the standard of play in Great Britain at an artificially low level.

One may ask why such a situation prevailed, especially in view of the intensive coaching and competitive system within the schools. Before one can even begin to appreciate the position, which to many people was quite illogical, one first has to understand the historical background to the development of Rugby Union Football, together with the basic philosophy which those who governed the game were so anxious to preserve.

The game was essentially for fun; it was part of a man's recreation; it was an opportunity for him to throw off the shackles and worry of work and express himself by means of uninhibited and joyful exercise. The game, too, had over the years developed a unique social atmosphere and a spirit which was much envied by other sports. In short, the game was different and those responsible for guiding its affairs wanted to keep it that way. An admirable sentiment, but not one it would seem which should automatically preclude any attempt to raise standards.

History shows that an early warning system had been established and it had produced the game's first crisis. I am referring to the events which saw the eventual establishment of the Rugby Football League. In the early eighteen-nineties clubs in the North of England had proposed that players should be recompensed for loss of earnings incurred through playing the game. This was a view which was bitterly opposed by the majority of clubs of the Rugby Football Union. In 1893 matters came to a head and a group of clubs in Lancashire and Yorkshire broke away from the Rugby Football Union and formed the Northern Union.

Those who opposed "broken-time" payments did so because they felt that it was the first step to professionalism. Their assessment was absolutely right. The Northern Union as it was originally called subsequently became the Rugby Football League and developed as a professional game. It is still mainly played as such in Lancashire and Yorkshire, but it must be acknowledged that Rugby League also has its amateur clubs. In no way however can they be compared with the strength and numbers in Rugby Union Football.

The bitter controversy which ensured in 1893 continued for many many years, and the Rugby Union authorities took punitive measures against anyone who sought to support the Rugby League game in any way. While the Home Unions have on many occasions been castigated for their attitude towards Rugby League Football, it was merely a reflection of the determination to ensure that Rugby Union Football survived as an amateur game.

This then was the background which created a situation where any organised effort among senior players to raise standards was regarded with suspicion. "You must not get too serious", was often the cry. One could appreciate the sentiment without agreeing with it. Those who made it did so in good faith because they were determined to maintain the status-quo. "Over my dead body", was often the reaction to pleas for change and it was this policy of "over-kill" which was such a limiting factor to the technical development of the game.

After World War II attitudes in sport were changing rapidly. They reflected a change in society and Rugby could not expect to remain immune. Before the war, in the middle thirties, there was much concern about the standard of fitness of the British people and the National Fitness Council was established. In truth it did little in the two years of its existence and on the outbreak of hostilities it folded up never to emerge again.

There was at this same time another organisation, also committed to the fitness cause, which was the creation of a remarkable woman, Phyllis Colson. It was the Central Council of Recreative Physical Training: founded in 1935 it carried on during the war and went from strength to strength. Significantly, in 1944 its name was changed to the Central Council of Physical Recreation (CCPR). It employed technical staff throughout its regions in England and in Wales and Northern Ireland. Scotland had its own Council.

I mention these details because the CCPR, as it was then, had a tremendous influence on the development of sport in this country, and especially on the promotion of governing body coaching schemes. Rugby Union Football was no exception as I hope to show, and the CCPR role in assisting, in particular the RFU and the WRU, is one of which relatively few people are aware. I must add, of course, that when the Sports Council became an executive body in 1972 it took over all CCPR assets including its staff and national sports centres. The CCPR still exists but in a vastly different form.

However, I wish to refer to the period after the war when the CCPR was organising many courses for leaders, coaches and players in a wide range of activities. Governing bodies were, often with CCPR encouragement and technical assistance, beginning to establish coaching schemes. Some were appointing national coaches in order to train teachers and club coaches. Such appointments as those of Geoffrey Dyson, Amateur Athletic Association, and Bob Anderson, Amateur Fencing Association, were made by means of grant-aid from the then Ministry of Education.

Early approaches to the Rugby Football Union met with only limited response, although the RFU held its first course—for schoolmasters—in 1954 at Bisham Abbey, a CCPR National Sports Centre. The position in Wales was rather different, for in 1950 the CCPR (Wales) was the prime mover in setting up a Rugby Coaching Scheme. Significantly it was not really a part of the Welsh Rugby Union, although members of the WRU General Committee were represented on the body which was called the Welsh Rugby Union Coaching Supervisory Sub-Committee. The Secretary of the Committee was Mr Ted Prater who was the Secretary to the CCPR Welsh Committee.

As the years went by, the WRU assumed a greater degree of control and authority over the Coaching Committee, until eventually it became a constituted committee of the Union. However, the CCPR (Wales) even then still continued to provide the secretary to the Coaching Committee, and so through its technical staff was able to stimulate the thinking on coaching within the WRU. This pattern existed until I became the WRU's first Coaching Organiser in 1967 and assumed responsibility for servicing the WRU Coaching Committee.

The most important date in coaching development in Wales was 1964. Wales went to South Africa and were heavily defeated internationally by 24 points to 3. This defeat had far-reaching repercussions, for at the 1964 Annual General Meeting of the WRU the General Committee was charged with the responsibility of "examining the state of Welsh Rugby and making recommendations for the future". The result was a working party on coaching. This in a sense saw the beginning of a nationally organised and accepted Coaching Scheme in Wales. The Working Party which laid down the foundations was inspired in particular by three men, Cliff Jones, a great outside half of the thirties, Alun Thomas, a 1955 Lion and Manager of the 1974 Lions, and Cadfan Davies, Secretary to the WRU Coaching Committee who was the CCPR's Senior Technical Representative in Wales. Their foresight and argument persuaded the WRU to adopt some quite revolutionary concepts, but perhaps the most dramatic was the acceptance of a paid official who would be responsible for the development of the coaching scheme. As I have already stated I began work in 1967 and so took part in a series of developments in which Wales could truly be said to be leading the Rugby world.

Paradoxically, up until that time I was much more familiar with the English scene. After leaving Loughborough College in 1951 I went as a physical education master to The King's School, Peterborough, and while I was there I played Rugby for London Welsh and Northampton. I played too for the East Midlands and even got a Final Welsh Trial, but was in contention with Cliff Morgan which made matters rather difficult!

However, as a physical educationist I was very keen on coaching, and I well remember writing to the late Col Douglas Prentice in 1955 when he was Secretary to the RFU and suggesting that perhaps the RFU should establish a coaching scheme with particular emphasis on the production of coaches. He replied to the effect that each constituent body was autonomous and responsible for its own affairs within the broad policy laid down by the RFU. I was to recollect that letter when soon afterwards I left Peterborough and went to Birmingham as a Technical Representative in the CCPR's West Midlands Region which covered Shropshire, Staffordshire, Herefordshire, Worcestershire and Warwickshire.

Naturally one of the sports for which I was responsible was Rugby Football, and by good fortune the President of the North Midlands Football Union, the late R. I. (Rusty) Scorer, was very keen on coaching. He gave me much encouragement and assistance and between us we revolutionised the approach to coaching in the North Midlands. Apart from the work with schoolboys, which many English Counties were doing, we began to organise courses for schoolmasters and eventually fitness courses for senior club players. From there we moved to conferences and courses for club coaches. In 1957 we introduced the North Midlands Coaching Certificate. Col Prentice was not too pleased because the North Midlands Football Union were really out of step with the rest of the country, but he was reminded by Rusty Scorer of the autonomy of the constituent bodies!

I had by now become the CCPR's Rugby "expert" not only in the Birmingham area but nationally as well. In those days the CCPR organised Coaching Holidays for people who wished to learn a new sport or improve at the one in which they already participated. I used to conduct national courses for players with the approval of the RFU, but really I wanted to work with teachers and coaches. The RFU were rather reluctant to organise national courses administered centrally; they doubted the demand. I persuaded the North Midlands Football Union that we should organise a four-day course for schoolmasters and give it national publicity. This we did in September 1958 and the response, 37 schoolmasters from 34 different schools as far apart as Eastbourne and Sedburgh, exploded the idea that there was no demand.

The following year the CCPR were given approval by the RFU to organise one-week courses for schoolmasters on a national scale, and we were on our way. I directed the courses and was helped by many friends I had either played with or played against and who had a coaching background. Gradually the RFU came more into the picture and began to exercise its authority and control. Eventually the courses became RFU Courses which were organised in co-operation with the CCPR. The RFU appointed its own Director and I acted as his Number One. The early courses in the sixties were directed by that splendid man Bernard Gadney, an outstanding scrum half for England and a person for whom I have the utmost regard.

The staff of these courses, among whom were Ian Beer, Bob MacEwen, Jeff Butterfield, Frank Sykes, Alan Ashcroft and Hywel Griffiths, became restless because we knew that organising a course even for 100 schoolmasters was not even scratching the surface. So we suggested to the RFU in 1963 that something much more fundamental was required, and that a conference should be held to see what ought to be done. The RFU, who had just appointed its first-ever coaching committee, readily agreed, and in fact in 1964 two conferences each lasting two and a half days were held at the CCPR's Lilleshall National Recreation Centre. The recommendations of those conferences were just as far-reaching in their way as those of the WRU Working Party, which coincidentally was set up at the same time.

The RFU Conferences made a number of proposals, but four were of real significance. They were that the RFU should appoint a full-time National Coach, establish a Coaching Advisory Panel, produce a new Coaching Manual and commission a series of visual aids. The idea of a National Coach was really a non-starter, at least to those of us near to RFU thinking. It was much too radical a concept. In fact, the proposal was watered down by the RFU and eventually J. P. (Jock) Walker was appointed as a Schools and Coaching Administrator. He was a man with vast experience in Physical Education and he had recently retired as the Senior Physical Education Organiser to Middlesex Education Authority, but as Jock himself said, "I am not a coach." Nevertheless, he gave great service to the RFU in a number of ways, most notably as the organiser of the Centenary Congress in 1970. The RFU eventually appointed Don Rutherford as its Technical Administrator in 1969, some five years after the idea was first mooted.

The other ideas were more readily accepted; a Coaching Advisory Panel was appointed and consisted of six people: Ian Beer (Chairman), Jeffrey Butterfield, Hywel Griffiths, Bob MacEwen, Mark Sugden and myself. Our first task was to produce a new Coaching Manual, and this proved an interesting if at times exasperating exercise. It is difficult enough to write a book on one's own, imagine six people trying to do it! Well, we succeeded, which was a real achievement. We even produced 12 filmlets illustrating various aspects of play as well as an additional

filmlet on Circuit Training. All this happened within two years of
the Lilleshall Conferences. Mention, too, must be made of Cyril
Gadney and Geoffrey Butler, both former RFU Presidents and in
their turn Chairmen of the RFU Coaching Committee. They gave
great encouragement and support to our efforts, invaluable
guidance and much sound advice.

The *Guide to Coaches* was published in March 1966 and it was
an historic document as well as being a best seller. It was
produced in pamphlet form, and perhaps Pamphlet No. 1 on
Attitudes and Fundamentals was the most crucial of all. It challenged much of the British Rugby philosophy and advocated some
drastic rethinking. Its appearance was timely, for the British Isles
Rugby team was just about to embark on a tour of Australia and
New Zealand. The facts are, that by any standards, it was a
disappointing tour and appeals for the implementation of some of
Pamphlet No. 1's thinking grew both in volume and number.

The 1966 Lions, however, did set a precedent in that an
Assistant Manager was appointed who had gained a reputation as
a coach—John Robins of Loughborough College. Unfortunately,
Robins, due to an ankle injury, was hospitalised for part of the
tour, but it must also be stated that the job specifications of the
management, vis-à-vis the captain, were neither clearly nor tightly
enough defined. It is probable, therefore, that even without injury
Robins would not have been able to exert the influence which his
expertise and background demanded. At least it was acknowledged that perhaps coaching could make a contribution even at
this level. The mistakes made in terms of defining responsibilities
were rectified for tours which were to follow.

I always thought that many people felt that the publication of
the *Guide to Coaches* was the end of the road. For me, it was the
beginning. It was merely the vehicle by which we could achieve so
much more. My CCPR experience, dealing with a complexity of
sports, had convinced me of one thing; a properly structured
coaching scheme for a major sport had to be professionally
organised. This was the action which I kept urging via meetings of

the RFU Coaching Advisory Panel. The need was obvious, there was a very big job to be done in "selling" the *Guide to Coaches*. The ideas had to be interpreted, courses had to be organised and this was plainly beyond the capacity of a person working in a voluntary capacity. Fortunately the CCPR had agreed to what almost amounted to my secondment to the RFU, but in any event this could only be a temporary arrangement. It is a fact that for the year following publication of the *Guide to Coaches* I conducted courses in Cheshire, Cumberland and Westmorland, Eastern Counties, East Midlands, Hampshire, Leicestershire, Middlesex, North Midlands and Warwickshire. I hasten to add that it was often a team effort when other members of the RFU Coaching Advisory Panel were also involved, but sometimes I worked by myself while my colleagues, too, were similarly committed. I mention this because I believe it completely vindicated the demand that such work should be co-ordinated and directed by a person who was employed full-time by the governing body.

The Welsh Rugby Union had responded to this idea, and they advertised for a "Coaching Organiser". I had campaigned so hard for so long that although by now I was a Senior Technical Representative with the CCPR I felt obliged to accept the challenge. I therefore applied for the post, was appointed and began working for the Welsh Rugby Union on 1st June 1967.

This then is a brief historical background to the establishment of a coaching system for Rugby Football in England and Wales. It is of course a highly personalised account. I make no apology for that because I happened to be directly involved in much of the early thinking. There *was* other work being done by other people, in schools mainly: Counties in England, too, often organised coaching courses for schoolboys at the beginning of each season. But no one was doing any really worthwhile work with teachers and coaches, and it was this above all else that was required if British Ruby was to up-date its game.

The fact that ideas became realities was not due to the efforts of any one individual. It was just that many people like myself were happily in a position to translate the aspirations of young men, who were no longer content to be second best, into positive action. The results are there for all to see. Rugby Union Football has never been stronger. Many more people are watching it and, even more important, many more people are playing it.

2 PHILOSOPHY

It may seem strange to some people to have a chapter on philosophy in a book on Rugby Football, but a coach's basic philosophy is truly reflected in the way in which he manages to persuade players to play the game. I must be honest and say that I know many coaches who, in the reputed words of the North American Indian, "speak with forked tongue". In modern parlance their deeds do not match their words.

Many people have asked me, "What kind of Rugby football do you advocate?" My answer is always the same: "Go and watch our national team play." One of the most remarkable features of Welsh Rugby over the past nine years has been the way in which the WRU Selection Committee and the National XV Coach have aligned themselves totally with the concepts which have been projected by the Coaching Committee. The fact that the WRU Selectors (and the National XV Coach is one of them) are nearly all members of the WRU Coaching Committee helps tremendously, because they are party to all the coaching decisions that are made.

There was one outstanding example of this co-operation in 1969, when the WRU Coaching Advisory Committee produced an excellent paper on *Back-Row Forward Play*. This document challenged the British system of play from the back row. It was, to say the least, controversial, but it was supported by the WRU Selectors who stated that in future their policy would be to look for right and left flankers as opposed to open-side and blind-side wing forwards. Clive Rowlands, who was the National XV Coach and a Selector, adopted this method and in my view it revolutionised Welsh forward play.

Our philosophy is a simple one. We want to win by scoring the greatest number of points that prevailing circumstances will permit. Wales has, in the past decade, always gone on to the field with that aim. We have not always won, but we have never betrayed our basic philosophy. Very few international teams can match that record. For many coaches and players winning becomes the be-all and end-all. We in Wales are always keen to win, but now we have a new attitude where winning becomes the first aim, not the only one.

I have been, over the years, highly critical of the New Zealand approach. Often magnificent teams have represented New Zealand but they did not realise their potential; they merely settled for winning. In my opinion that is nowhere near enough. Winning is the beginning, not the end. Coaching is concerned with the pursuit of excellence, and the coach has to influence his players into thinking this way because only then will he produce a game of high quality involving all fifteen players.

The England/Wales match at Twickenham in 1976 was a practical example of what I mean. Wales won by 21 points to 9; the biggest margin of victory ever at Twickenham. Yet when I went into the dressing-room after the game you would have thought we had lost. The players were disappointed because they knew that they had not played as well as they could. In an interview after the game John Dawes, the National XV Coach, said that Wales had played badly and was criticised for his remarks. It was felt that he was being ungracious to England's effort.

If you knew John Dawes as well as I do, then you would know that ungraciousness is not a part of his make-up. He is a very honest person, who believes in quality Rugby football but also feels that we should not kid ourselves. How easy it would have been to say what a great victory (which it was) and what a great game (which it wasn't). He said later that Wales, by her own high standards, played badly. He said too that he did not set the standards, the players themselves did. Personally, I felt elated because now we had produced a group of players for whom winning was not enough, they also had to win well.

Of course there are those who say that we have set too high a standard, and that we are expecting perfection every time, but as Dawes said, it is the players themselves who set the standards. Trying to play positive Rugby against those who are dedicated to stopping you is a part of the challenge, and complete victory, when it comes, is very sweet. In this context, merely settling for winning is a soft option.

Words like "philosophy" and "attitude" often mean little to players and coaches. One of my main functions is to train coaches, and in this work I rely very much on the adage "success through simplicity". In effect it means that, even though I use words like "philosophy" and "attitude", I must make them meaningful terms. For if I cannot make coaches understand, what chance is there that they in their turn will make players understand? I therefore try to define such terms in a simple way.

Having stated then, that playing positive effective football is part of our philosophy, I try to define "positive" and "effective" so that there is no doubt about what our aim is. Positiveness is causing things to happen. A team can be positive in attack; it tries to create situations and capitalise on them. Equally it can be positive in defence; by putting the opposition under pressure it can cause them to make mistakes. The negative way is to wait for things to happen. This approach is identified with the side which lives like a parasite on the mistakes of others. Such an approach can produce a limited amount of success, but problems arise when this kind of side meets a team whose mistakes are minimal.

Effective football really means playing the game in your opponents' part of the field and not in your own. Open football, 15-man football, is so often misinterpreted. To many people it means throwing the ball about with gay abandon. This is a total misconception. A team must learn to be effective, and in order to do so players need to use their total range of skills which often means kicking as well as passing. Open football which is ineffective is bad football, and every player in a team must be made aware of this fact.

This is not quite the total picture, because the aim must not only be to play positive effective football but to do so within the Laws of the game. When coaches say, as they often do, "We must not give away penalties", the cynic says that what they really mean is that they must not get caught. I do not subscribe to this view. I accept that there are players who cheat, but there are an even greater number who technically are cheating but who, in truth, are really playing to the limits which the referees set. The purist will often say that players by playing to the referee are not accepting the Laws at face value. Of course they are not, and no player should be expected to do so. The Laws of the game are complicated to say the least, and often subject to different interpretations. Players must be prepared to play by the Laws as interpreted by each individual referee, to accept each decision without hesitation and certainly without question. In this area in particular can be seen the discipline of a team, and again discipline is so often a reflection of attitudes which a coach has developed in a side.

I am, of course, talking about technical infringements—in no way, whatever the interpretations of a referee, would I condone foul play and thuggery. This is the certain way to disaster for the team and the game. Players who take part in Rugby football do so in the knowledge that it is a hard game, involving a lot of physical contact which is allowed for within the laws of the game. No player should ever be subjected to risks which are outside the Laws of the game, and coaches, who can contribute the greatest good to the game, must never ever lose sight of this indisputable fact.

So far, although I have mentioned coaching, I have said little about the coach. Coaching after all is only the means by which the coach expresses himself. Perhaps, therefore, attention should be focussed on the coach. What for instance are the qualities needed to become a good coach? There are naturally many factors which go to make a successful coach but three qualities stand out above all others. The first is attitude—a coach must have the right attitude towards the game. Well, what is the right attitude? Certainly he must have respect for the game and for those who play it. He must be positive in his approach and he must want his team to play positive, effective football. These objectives should not be pipe-dreams, but targets which are worth striving for, and there are many coaches about now who have proved that they are attainable.

Second, a coach must have technical knowledge; he must be able to discuss the game intelligently with players. In this respect he must have a good background in technique and skill. He must be able to assess, analyse and correct the mistakes which he sees, but above all he must have humility, because one thing is certain—a coach will learn as much from players as they will learn from him.

Third, a coach needs to be able to motivate and stimulate others, and this is the most important quality of all. A coach who cannot influence players is nothing. It is of little use having superb attitude and great depth of technical knowledge if a coach lacks the ability to communicate. It is communication which is the real tool of a coach, and here one is really talking about personality. This is the factor which makes coaching an art rather than a science. A coach has to be something of a psychologist, and the higher the standard of the players then the more perceptive a coach needs to be.

In educational circles there is a saying, "If you want to teach John Latin, then you not only have to know Latin, you also have to know John." This was never more true than in Rugby football. It is my privilege to be closely associated with three great coaches: Clive Rowlands (Welsh National Team Coach 1968–74), Carwyn James (British Lions Coach 1971) and John Dawes (the present Welsh National Team Coach). They are all great personalities in their own right, they have all been extremely successful and yet they are all different.

The area, in my view, where they are most effective is in that of influence and motivation. Clive Rowlands when coaching the National XV was most astute in dealing with players as individuals; he knew those he had to bully and those he had to coax. He got some amazing reactions in his celebrated team talks, but as Clive would say on these occasions, "I'll leave Barry (John) alone because he'll only start to laugh!"

Carwyn James, much more academic in his approach but equally effective, is a great listener. He weighs up the various views and then makes his own decisions. He is a good delegator and believes in sharing responsibility among players and using their expertise.

John Dawes has a great start among international players. He is close enough to the game to be highly respected as a captain and a player, and obviously this alone makes his coaching task much easier. He has many great qualities, not least that of being a meticulous preparer of coaching sessions. Players do not have a chance to become bored. National Squad Sessions, even after a hard match the day before, are usually stimulating experiences under John's thoughtful direction.

One quality all three of them possess is the ability to develop a rapport with the team captain. Recently, various people, including none other than Dr Danie Craven of South Africa, have expressed concern at the apparent demise of the captain's role in Rugby football. It is not a view which I share, although I will admit that it is a danger inherent in the coaching situation and we must be aware of it.

We must first of all appreciate that not all that takes place under the guise of coaching is necessarily good. We can have bad coaches just as easily as we can have bad players, bad referees and, yes, even bad captains! With the emergence of the coach it is inevitable that the authority and control of the captain would diminish. Is this necessarily bad for the game? To those who suggest that it is I would ask the question, "What makes the captain's position so sacrosanct?" The advent of the coach means that the responsibility for directing a team's effort can be shared, and I have always felt coach and captain are partners in a joint effort. The coach directs the off-field operation while the captain assumes control on the field. Unless the two act in concert then there can be little chance of success. In situations where there is no rapport between coach and captain, the matter is best resolved by one or the other relinquishing his position. I have known this situation arise in several clubs. Until the matter was settled, the uneasy relationship between coach and captain often spilled over on to the playing field and was reflected in the team's performance.

However, let us be positive and say that coach and captain must be on the same wavelength if a team is to stand any chance of realising its potential. Both of them have a contribution to make towards the development of the game, and each must understand his role within the game.

Those who cannot accept the challenge, advocate appointing a captain who also coaches the team. This is dodging the issue and a complete negation of coaching philosophy. Who coaches the captain? Where is the objective view? How can a captain assess a situation in which he is also participating? There are some exceptional people who have made a brave attempt at combining the two jobs. John Dawes did it successfully with London Welsh, but it is not an answer which he would advocate.

Many would argue, of course, that I am so committed to "coaching" that I too cannot really present an objective view. This may be true, because I believe the future of the game is very much bound up with the future of coaching. Coaches have a tremendous influence on the way in which the game is played. They are responsible for projecting the image of Rugby football, and in a society where many interests are competing for the time and enthusiasm of young men it is vital that a good image emerges. The responsibility therefore is a heavy one, and that is why Rugby Unions through their Coaching Schemes should be trying to produce men as coaches whose attitude is beyond reproach; men with boldness and imagination who respect the great tradition and spirit of Rugby football and at the same time strive to reach new and better standards in the eternal pursuit of excellence.

3 STRUCTURE

During the first session of every course for coaches I try to indicate where coaching fits into the framework of Rugby football. I make two statements to illustrate my argument: "Coaching and the game are one and the same", and "Coaching is only a part of the game". These points are made because they reflect totally opposed views; those who think of coaching in isolation from the game and those who think that in coaching lies the answer to all the problems which are met in the game.

I came across the former very soon after my appointment to the WRU. Those early days were concerned with promoting concepts about the game and how coaching could help achieve them. Often club secretaries would ring me up and ask if I could go and give a talk about coaching. My answer was always the same, "No, but I will come and talk about Rugby football." In this way I tried to demonstrate that coaching was not an end in itself, it was merely the means to an end which I took to be a higher quality of Rugby football.

This is not to say that every player can be an international. It is said that one cannot put in what God left out, and if a coach has poor material to work with there is no way in which he can produce excellence. However, we must talk relatively and I am convinced that every player at whatever level can become better, and consequently that every team can improve. Improvement brings enjoyment and I can think of no better reason for wanting to play Rugby.

In effect, I am saying that coaching has its part to play within the structure of the game but coaching, too, must have its own structure if its contribution is to be an on-going process. It must be a structure which is defined at national, provincial/county/

district and club level. The organisation of coaching must be seen to be part of the democratic process. Particular difficulties can ensue if this is not the case.

I speak from experience because I was in precisely this position. I referred earlier to my work in the North Midlands Football Union with Rusty Scorer who was the President. There was a Coaching Committee of sorts but it never met. Rusty Scorer and I would meet and agree a course of action. He would then tell the Executive Committee and that was that. In the beginning I was quite satisfied because I wanted to get action, but, essential though this was, it was a short-term objective. In the long term there had to be a structure which was much more tightly defined. There had to be a properly constituted committee which was functioning correctly and was planning for the future. But this was the late fifties and many people did not even see the need for coaching, let alone setting up committees to promote it.

It was a long hard struggle and I think it took me nearly ten years to achieve what was necessary. If prior to this time I had left the area, the work I had done would have collapsed like a pack of cards because it was centred on me as an individual. All the effort would have been to no avail. As it happened, a proper Coaching Committee was eventually established with its own Chairman and Secretary, and I merely became the CCPR man who liaised with it. I did in fact leave shortly afterwards, but there was no interruption in the work that was being done, because the coaching structure had been properly established.

Let us first look at coaching structures at various levels. I will outline the Welsh Rugby Union situation because obviously it is the one I know best and the one I would recommend. I must begin by saying that as far as Rugby is concerned, and Welsh Rugby in particular, I believe in centralisation. A centralised administration and structure makes for much more control. Wales is particularly fortunate because it is a small country and centralisation is easy to achieve.

I feel that the very strength of English Rugby with its great number of clubs and players is also its weakness. It took the RFU a long time to bring out a policy statement on coaching. This was essential, otherwise each constituent body would develop in its own way and there could be as many different Coaching Schemes as there were constituent bodies. South Africa is now in that situation. Four of its Provincial Unions have appointed full-time people to develop coaching schemes. Pieter Pelser in the Transvaal has been working there for several years. How difficult it will be when the South African Rugby Board decide to appoint a man to direct South Africa's coaching affairs. There will be a minimum of four well-established coaching schemes with perhaps different aims, ideas and objectives. Yet a National Scheme is something which must happen if South Africa is to up-date its game.

It will be perhaps helpful to understand the Welsh scene if I state my own particular Terms of Reference, for it will indicate the responsibility and the areas to be covered.

In General: to be responsible to the Welsh Rugby Union through the Secretary and the Coaching Committee for all matters relating to coaching and the development of the game of Rugby Union Football in Wales.

In Particular: 1. Liaison with officials of the Sports Council for Wales, Education Authorities, University Colleges, Colleges of Education and all clubs and affiliated organisations;

2. Responsibility for proffering advice to any member club wishing to apply for financial assistance from any body empowered to give such assistance for the development or purchase of playing and other facilities;

3. Responsibility for training Staff, Senior and Club Coaches and advising and assisting all bodies concerned with the training of coaches, teachers and referees of Rugby Union Football;

4. Acting as Secretary to the Coaching and Advisory

Committees with responsibility for producing Minutes and Reports for information and consideration of the WRU General Committee;

5. Responsibility for arranging courses and conferences for coaches, players and referees;

6. Keeping abreast of all developments in the game of Rugby Union Football and ensuring that all coaches are kept informed of such developments;

7. Arranging for the conduct of courses leading to the Coaching Award and Referees' Certificate and arranging examinations therefore;

8. Maintaining a Register of Coaches appointed by the Welsh Rugby Union operating in Wales and elsewhere;

9. Responsibility for the Welsh Rugby Union's library of films and technical books and for their allocation and distribution;

10. Responsibility for developing a visual aids section of loops and film strips for schools and clubs.

It can be seen fairly quickly that these terms of reference are wide ranging and cover all aspects of the technical development of the game. However wide-ranging they may be, they do not in fact cover all the areas of the work which I do on behalf of the Union. There is a great deal of other work concerned with the development and promotion of the game for which I have been given responsibility. For example I am the Secretary to the Under-19 Working Party, a Committee discussing the future of Under-19 Rugby in Wales and from which Mini-Rugby first emanated. I serve, too, on the Union's Competition Sub-Committee. I mention these facts to illustrate the various ways in which a full-time technical person can be used in order to develop the game.

After I had been in office some four or five years it became obvious that the Union needed further full-time technical staff in its coaching department, and in September 1973 J. Malcolm Lewis began work as the WRU Assistant Coaching Organiser.

His presence made a big difference because it meant that our service in the field—to education authorities, colleges and universities—could be increased. The Union benefits from very generous grant-aid in relation to its coaching programme from the Sports Council for Wales. It aids the salaries of coaching staff, office administration and attendance at courses and conferences for coaches and players.

The Union's technical staff are responsible to the WRU Coaching Committee whose recommendations are in turn subject to ratification by the WRU General Committee. In 1975 there was some rationalisation of the WRU's various committees in an attempt to reduce the demand on individuals. The result was a combining of the Coaching and Laws Committees. The amalgamation appears to be working satisfactorily. The original intention was to bring in the Referees Committee as well and call the resultant Committee the WRU Technical Committee. However, it was not possible at that time. I must say, however, that it is worthy of further consideration in the future.

Very often one of the weaknesses apparent in the structure of many governing bodies of sport is the inability of those who are closest to the sport in a technical sense to get their views considered. Rugby football, at least in the four Home Unions, has got over this problem in a unique and most acceptable manner. Coaching Advisory Committees or Panels have been appointed, whose function is to advise the Coaching Committees on technical matters relating to the development of the game.

The idea originated in England and Wales in 1964, coincidently as far as I am aware, and Scotland and Ireland followed suit at a later date. This means that coaches, players or men with a special background or expertise can make a real contribution to a Union's thinking without having to be a member of a particular Executive Committee.

In Wales the Coaching Advisory Committee is composed of a Chairman and Vice-Chairman, who must be members of the WRU General Committee, together with eight members who are selected because of their experience and background and who are not WRU Committee members. The Advisory Committee is completed by the addition of an assessor from the Sports Council for Wales, and the Union's two technical staff. The Assistant Coaching Organiser acts as the Secretary to this Committee. Cliff Jones was the first Chairman of the WRU Coaching Advisory Committee. He was then followed by Alun Thomas who served for two terms of three years. The present Chairman is Clive Rowlands, with John Dawes as his deputy.

The contribution of the Coaching Advisory Committee to Welsh thinking in Rugby football over the past ten years has been immense, and the following examples illustrate very clearly the range and depth of discussion:

(i) The WRU Back-Row paper (1968)
(ii) A paper on Competitive Rugby in Wales (1968)
(iii) The technical details relating to Mini-Rugby (1971)
(iv) The WRU Line-out paper (1975)
(v) The WRU Back-Play paper (1976).

What the above list cannot do, however, is indicate the dedication and passionate argument which those who have served the Coaching Advisory Committee have brought to each specific area studied.

Implicit in the term "Coaching Scheme" is the fact that there must be coaches. In the Welsh Rugby Union there are three grades of coach:

1. Staff Coach—one who is capable of coaching at the highest level and conducting courses for coaches and players, and assessing coaches for the WRU Coaching Award;

2. Senior Coach—one who is capable of coaching at district/county level and/or conducting courses for players and assisting on courses for coaches;

3. Coach—one who is capable of coaching at club or school level.

If persons are going to be designated as coaches then there has to be some acceptable method of assessing them. In Wales we have the WRU Coaching Award which can only be attained by attending a WRU Coaching Award Assessment Coarse lasting a week. Successful candidates who, apart from continual assessment during the week, are required to complete a written and practical examination, are placed on the WRU Register of Coaches. The Register is revised every three years and those coaches who do not reply or cannot produce evidence of coaching have their names deleted. In this way we keep a list of coaches who are all, as near as is practically possible, active in the field.

The basic Coaching Award is the only coaching grade in which it is possible to qualify by attending a course and passing an examination. Staff and Senior Coaches are appointments made by invitation only. This is deliberate policy because it is often too easy for coaches in some sports to pass examinations without having the relevant experience, and sometimes with a minimum of coaching commitment. WRU Staff and Senior Coaches have all got a record of proven coaching achievement, and even more important are prepared to assist in furthering the Union's coaching development by conducting courses etc. Such appointments last for three years and the matter of re-appointment is then considered by the Coaching Committee.

This then is the basic structure of coaching within the Welsh Rugby Union. The overall policy is decided by the WRU Coaching Committee (subject to the approval of the WRU General Committee), with advice from the WRU Coaching Advisory Committee. The responsibility for directing and carrying out this policy lies with the Union's full-time technical staff.

The picture would appear very rosy. Few would argue that the national pattern is not well-structured. I honestly believe that this is one of the reasons—not the only one—for the success of the Welsh national team over the past decade, but there is always the danger of becoming complacent and past events have proven that complacency forever lurks at the door of British Rugby. My contention is that there is still a long way to go in Welsh and British Rugby in order to make the most of what we have got.

The big challenge lies within the clubs. Wales can point to an adequate coaching structure at national level but this is not true of the club scene. If coaching is to make its greatest impact then it must also be structured within clubs. In the vast majority of cases this is quite clearly not being done. Clubs are usually content to have the services of a coach but all too often he operates in a vacuum—he has no help and no direct access to the club committee.

Coaches themselves are just as much to blame as committees. There are those who think that they do not need assistance: an unrealistic view. There are others who would resent it because they feel that it might undermine their authority. Many coaches also take the view that they should only be concerned with players, and that serving on, or associating with, committees takes away from the time that can be spent with players. This may be so but it is through committees that policy decisions are taken and these can quite often have a direct effect on the coaching situation.

The answer to the problem lies in a properly structured coaching system within each club. I strongly recommend that every club should have its own coaching committee. Its function would be to be responsible for all matters relating to coaching, to liaise with the Club General Committee and to create the kind of environment which would allow coaches to work most effectively. Such a committee would ensure that the facilities and equipment available for coaching were adequate, but most of all it would pursue a policy in relation to the training of coaches. This could be achieved internally within the club by discussion and practical sessions, and meetings at the beginning of the club's preparation for a new season to discuss playing policy, to outline objectives and make plans for their achievement would be most valuable. Suitable people could be earmarked for attendance at national courses for the training of coaches.

A system of this kind is essential if coaching within a club is to be an on-going process. Far too many clubs live a hand-to-mouth existence as far as coaches are concerned. Some clubs have only one coach: while he is there everyone is satisfied, but coaches, like players and referees, do not go on for ever. A coach may decide to retire, he may leave the district or indeed the club may decide to terminate the relationship. In any event and for whatever reason, there is often no ready-made successor and as far as the club is concerned, it is back to "Square One" and the search begins for a replacement.

This in itself is no simple matter because training a coach takes time, and developing his potential takes even longer. The answer must be in careful planning in the production and development of coaches rather in the same way that one tries to develop players. I am often asked by club secretaries for a coach to take over a team. This is not my function. There is no way in which I can produce people like rabbits out of a hat. My·work is concerned with trying to assist those who are put forward by the clubs. They can be made more effective as coaches, but initially it is the clubs and schools which must produce those who wish to make a contribution to the game through coaching. A properly structured coaching system within the clubs would seem at least the best chance of achieving such an objective.

If, of course, in a big Union like the RFU there is another stratum between Union and Club such as a province, state, county or district, then the same kind of coaching structure would need to be created at that level. I still believe, however, that the overall scheme must be overseen by the Union, otherwise we will get the kind of fragmentation which is so typical in British Sport and so wasteful of effort.

4   ORGANISATION

Standards in Rugby football are governed by three factors: Participation, Competition and Coaching. They are three vital areas in the quest for excellence. I regard them as the corner-stones of Rugby development. They can be compared with the three-legged stool, take one leg away and the stool collapses. One must ensure through careful organisation that there is balanced development. My brief in this book is to deal with the coaching scene, but I do make some observations on the other "legs" in Section IV.

In the same way that we should have a balanced programme in the total development of the game, so should we also treat coaching. This is done in Wales and we arrange courses for coaches, players and referees at all levels. The term "at all levels" is extremely important because coaching should be ultimately concerned with raising the overall standard of the game. In doing so it will make for greater enjoyment both on the side of participants— be they coaches, players or referees—and on the side of those who watch—be they club officials, members or ordinary spectators.

We try through our organisation to monitor the progress of coaches, players and referees. The system is not by any means perfect, but it does make an attempt in the first place to raise the overall standard and secondly to ensure that promising talent is allowed to develop its potential.

COACHES
It is difficult to know precisely where to begin, but let me start with the organisation which exists to train coaches. I think then that the other areas will fall into place more easily. One of the

early decisions relating to coaching was that if we were to have a
Coaching Scheme then *ipso facto* we had to have coaches. It
therefore followed that we had to train coaches, and if at the end
of a period of training people wanted to call themselves "WRU
Coaches" then an acceptable method of assessing their capability
had to be devised. Mere attendance at a course was not sufficient
because there would be both good and poor coaches. A poor
coach could do much harm to the Coaching Scheme, so if he
failed to reach the required standard he should not be entitled to
call himself "WRU Coach". The WRU Coaching Award is only
granted to those people who successfully attend a WRU Coaching
Award Assessment Course. The course lasts one week and is
residential. Residence is not compulsory but it is encouraged
because of the long hours which are worked each day. As the title
of the course suggests, it is one where each coach is being continually assessed by the Staff Coach in charge of his group. This
assessment is then supplemented by an independent practical
examination, and a written paper at the end of the week. The
thought of a written paper often puts off potential coaches, but I
explain that the biggest weighting is given to practical coaching
performance and that the written paper is devised in such a way
that one does not need a degree in English to be able to answer it!
Such assurances usually swing the balance in favour of attendance
at a course.

The WRU have had a Coaching Award since 1950, but while
the restructuring was taking place between 1964 and 1967 the
Award was suspended. It was revived again in 1968 in a new
form. In the days of the old Coaching Award many courses for
coaches were held and many coaches qualified. For the most part
they attended courses as individuals, they were not attached to
any particular club and on qualifying as a coach they had nowhere to go. This was largely because the Coaching Scheme had
been superimposed on the Rugby scene without really being part
of it.

There was, however, in 1964 a total transformation because the

WRU recommended that every club should have a coach, and the coach immediately had status. Maybe in the beginning it was tenuous but at least it was a step in the right direction. Nowadays on courses, individuals as such are a rarity; most people attending courses for coaches are sent by clubs. This has one big plus factor in its favour, for nearly all those people sent by clubs turn out to be strong on personality. Earlier I wrote of the qualities of a coach; attitude, technical know-how and the ability to motivate. On a course we can influence attitude, we can improve technical know-how but there is little that can be done to affect personality, and this is the factor which enables a person to motivate.

Clubs by their selection, whether deliberate or not, are making a big contribution to the development of coaches by ensuring that the most important quality, and the one most difficult to acquire, is already present in those who come on courses. The rest is relatively easy; to influence attitude, give information, teach coaching method, develop confidence. Then you have the makings of a coach.

The last sentences really sum up a WRU Coaching Award Assessment Course in a nutshell. I remember discussing the training of coaches with Ivan Vodanovich, the All Black Coach, when I was in New Zealand in 1970. He talked about some of their courses lasting a whole day or even two days! He was astounded when I told him WRU Courses lasted a week. He thought it was very "scientific". I do not know about that but they are certainly systematic. I suppose that during the last 21 years I have conducted more courses for coaches and players than any other person anywhere. I know, too, that the courses which I direct now bear almost no resemblance to those I did in my early coaching days. I have learnt as I have gone along, much of it from other people, for which I am extremely grateful.

One of the biggest weaknesses in the many coaches' courses which I have seen is a gross assumption which is made. People are often "talked at". Heads are filled with ideas but the ideas are never translated into the practical situation. The assumption is that if people have the information they will be able to impart it, whether it be a technique or a particular coaching method. We must recognise the reality of the situation. A man may come on a course for coaches whose main qualifications for attending the course are that he is willing, most important, and that he has a good playing background. Perhaps, because he was a centre, he has never been near a scrum, does not know what it is like to pack in the front row, or perhaps he has never stood in front of a group of players and told them what to do.

These are big gaps in his Rugby education and the least a course can do is to try to rectify these deficiencies. A WRU Course does precisely this. A programme of a typical course is drawn up in Fig. 1. In it we try to influence attitude, not only in the opening session called "The Concept" but throughout the whole course. It is done in a variety of ways even by insisting on effort in practical sessions, by the taking down of information and by punctuality at all times. A coach without discipline is lacking a fundamental coaching tool.

Information is fed relating to individual, unit and team skills; methods of acquiring and improving basic fitness are explained and practised. Coaches are encouraged, too, to improve their own personal performance. It all adds up to credibility in the end. There are sessions which are designated "Mutual Coaching". The coaches coach each other, and criticise each other afterwards. In the Coaching Practice sessions we arrange for 60 to 80 boys to come along as guinea pigs. Every coach is given a coaching task. They are given the unique opportunity of being put in a fairly realistic coaching situation and of being helped to improve their performance by colleagues and staff.

Each course is usually directed either by myself or my colleague Malcolm Lewis, the WRU Assistant Coaching Organiser. We normally have the help of three Staff Coaches plus other staff to give specialist lectures on fitness, refereeing, Rugby injuries etc. The course is then divided into three groups, each group under the control of a Staff Coach. They stay together for a week and they

A TYPICAL WRU COACHING AWARD ASSESSMENT COURSE

	9.30–10.45 a.m.	11.15 a.m.–12.30 p.m.	2.15–3.30 p.m.	3.45–4.45 p.m.	4.45–5.30 p.m.	7.00–8.30 p.m.
Saturday			The Concept	Basic Coaching: Theme—the development of skill	Film	
Sunday	Basic Coaching: Theme—handling	Basic Coaching: Theme—contact and support	Basic Coaching: Theme—scrum possession	Basic Coaching: Theme—scrum possession	Group Seminars	Rugby Injuries
Monday	Mutual Coaching and Feed back	Basic Coaching: Theme—line-out possession	Basic Coaching: Theme—ruck and maul	Mutual Coaching	Introducing the game	Mini-Rugby film
Tuesday	Feed back and Mutual Coaching	Basic Coaching: Theme—back play	Coaching Practice	Coaching Practice	Group Seminars	The Art of Teaching/Coaching
Wednesday	Mutual Coaching and Feed back	The Laws in relation to Coaching	Coaching Practice	Coaching Practice	The Organised Coaching Session	The Search for Fitness
Thursday	Mutual Coaching and Feed back	The Laws in relation to Coaching	Coaching Practice	Coaching Practice	Group Seminars	WRU Coaching Award—written paper
Friday	Coaching Assessment Preparation	Coaching Assessment	Coaching Assessment	Coaching Assessment	Final discussion	

Fig. 1.

Notes: 1. Visual Aids will be used extensively during the week.
During many of the practical sessions some time will be devoted to "Individual Skill Clinics".

get to know each other very well. I always say at the beginning of
every course that those attending are in for a unique Rugby
experience. Some coaches have come to me later and said that the
course changed their total Rugby thinking. Perhaps it can be best
summed up by Nelie Smith (Springbok Selector and Captain in
1964). He attended one of our courses as an observer in 1973—
many overseas Unions send observers to WRU Courses—and at
the end of the course he said that he had paid his own expenses to
come from South Africa to Wales. When he got back people
would ask him was it worth it, and Nelie said "I shall tell them
that it is the best investment I have ever made." Coming from a
man involved in the Real Estate business that was praise indeed.

Those who are successful on the course—the failure rate is in
the order of 20 per cent—are appointed to the WRU Register of
Coaches. We do not, however, then forget about them. We keep in
regular contact by dispersing information and by an annual
Conference for WRU Coaches. This takes place over a weekend
in the close season. We assemble on a Friday evening and disperse
on the following Sunday around tea-time. The programme is
arranged in such a way that the coaches are exposed to new ideas
on coaching and training. International coaches from other
Unions are invited. International players too have a contribution
to make; the players' view is often taken for granted. Discussions
are held on a variety of common problems; views are exchanged
and sometimes grievances aired. The greatest bonus, however,
comes from bringing coaches in all parts of Wales together and
making them feel a part of Welsh Rugby. They go away
stimulated and ready to meet the challenge of the new season. This
is just one way in which we can ensure that we have conformity,
within a wide and flexible framework, and adherence to a basic
Welsh pattern of play.

This work is only part of the story, for we are here dealing only
with WRU Coaches who are qualified. There are many more
teachers and coaches working below this level, and they too are
given help. Special day courses are organised for coaches from

the Welsh Districts Rugby Union (formerly Welsh Junior Rugby Union); lecture-demonstrations are given at individual clubs, and other clubs in the locality are invited to attend. Coaches of all grades are invited to attend National Squad sessions so that they can see the kind of work which the National XV Coach does with international players. Some time ago Cliff Jones, Chairman of the WRU Coaching/Laws Committee, made an interesting and significant observation. He had attended a National Squad session in the Afan Lido, Port Talbot, on a Sunday. The following day he went to Fishguard on business. In the evening he went to Fishguard Rugby Club and watched a club practice evening. He said that apart from the different faces it was a replica of the National Squad session.

The WRU also has developed a very close link with colleges, universities and education authorities. A special coaching award for students in colleges and universities has been devised. Groups of students are not allowed to enter for the WRU Coaching Award, although they can apply as individuals. The WRU, in order to give a service, established a Students' Coaching Certificate which covers the basic elements of teaching, coaching and refereeing Rugby football in schools. It is not necessary for students to attend a course: the normal college Rugby programme is regarded as sufficient background. Many of the colleges, however, do arrange special courses directed either by the WRU Technical Staff or by Staff Coaches.

The co-operation with local education authorities is excellent: many in-service courses are arranged for teachers, sometimes the emphasis will be on teaching the game in the primary school, and on other occasions the aim will be to deal with the secondary school level. Most of these courses are of short duration, rarely lasting more than two days, but they do prove to be a fruitful source of recruitment for full WRU Assessment Courses. The one-week assessment course has now been running for six years. Initially there was one course a year, but now we are organising three and there is usually a waiting list. The maximum accepted on any one course is 27, and this limit is set by the number which it is possible to examine on the last day of the course. The WRU Register of Coaches was established in 1968 and there are now something like 300 coaches on it, all working hard in schools and clubs.

Coaches of course motivate players, and when there are 300 working on the same basic principles they can have a tremendous impact which is felt at all levels. This is the big bonus of centralisation: all these coaches derive from the same source. They have all attended WRU Coaching courses and have been exposed to the same philosophy and ideas. One criticism that is sometimes levelled is that the system is like a sausage machine and makes for stereotyping. Nothing could be further from the truth. Coaches who attend courses are stimulated to think; they are presented with options; they are given a broad canvas. How they fill in the detail is a matter which each coach must decide for himself.

PLAYERS

We know for certain that thousands of players in Wales are working to a basic Welsh pattern, whether it be in school or club. This is a system which enables those players with talent to come through to the top, but it does not just happen, we have to work at it. Apart from the work which goes on in clubs and schools, organisations such as the Cardiff and District Schools Rugby Union, Pontypridd and District SRU, Newport and District SRU arrange courses at the beginning of each season for their most promising players. On a broad front some of the local education authorities such as Mid and West Glamorgan organise courses for players both at Under-19 and Under-15 level. In all cases the WRU Technical Staff play some kind of role, either in advising on suitable coaches or by actually directing the course themselves.

In effect this produces a sifting process for what takes place at national level. The Union arranges courses for players at the various levels under 19 years of age. The normal pattern is to have two open courses: both last one week and are residential. One is for players 13 and 14 years (i.e. Under 15), and the other is for players 15 to 18 (i.e. Under 19). "Open" signifies that any player within the age range can apply, irrespective of his experience and background. Every player therefore gets the opportunity of improving his ability in the game. There are about 120 places made available in this way, and of course the Under-19 group caters for both School and Youth Union players.

As well as the "open" courses we also arrange courses for selected players, at Schools level, Under-19 and Under-15, and at Youth level, Under-19. One course for 70 players combines School and Youth Union players at Under-19. The players are selected by the respective Unions and the course takes place at the beginning of August. It lasts one week and again is residential. The Under-15 course is a three-day residential course immediately after Christmas and caters for about 45 players. The standard on all these courses is invariably high, for they form the basis of the National Squad in that particular age group for that season. Subsequently, of course, coaching sessions are held during the season for each age-group National Squad. It has happened that the Schools' Under-19 squad has coincidently been present for a squad session when the senior Welsh National Squad had also been meeting. The opportunity is not wasted, at lunchtime both squads are brought together and the younger players pick their opposite number in the senior squad and they chat together. It is very worthwhile. It also has its amusing sidelines, Bobby Windsor the Welsh Hooker once told me after one of the "chats" that he had learnt a lot!

Fig. 2 sets out the programme which has been developed on players' courses over the years. The purpose of the course is to give young players the opportunity of developing their potential within the team environment. We aim also to give them a better understanding of the game. We achieve our objectives in a variety of ways. Each course is divided into two groups, each of about 35 players. In the open courses we are lucky in that all positions are

A TYPICAL WRU COURSE FOR SELECTED PLAYERS

	9.30–10.00 a.m.	10.00–10.45 a.m.	11.00 a.m.–12.30 p.m.	2.30–4.00 p.m.	4.30–5.30 p.m.	7.30 p.m.
Sunday	Tests and Measurement Session		Principles of Play	Assessment Session	Recreational Period—WSRU. Basic Conditioning—WYRU.	Films and discussion
Monday	Warm-up Grids—Go Forward	Basic Coaching: Scrum Back Play from Scrum	Basic Coaching: Ruck and Maul Back Play from Ruck and Maul	Team Practice	Recreational Period—WYRU. Weight Training—WSRU.	Films and discussion
Tuesday	Warm-up Grids—Support	Basic Coaching: Scrum Back Play from Scrum	Basic Coaching: Line-out Back Play from Line-out	Team Practice	Weight Training—WYRU. Basic Conditioning—WSRU.	Films and discussion
Wednesday	Warm-up Grids—Continuity	Individual Skill Clinics	Team Practice	Free	Free	Free
Thursday	Warm-up Grids—Pressure	Individual Skill Clinics	Laws Forum	Match Preparation	Free	Films and discussion
Friday	Warm-up Grids—Contact	Test and Measurement Results	Match	Match Analysis and Discussion	Free	

Fig. 2.

covered fairly evenly, so we get roughly two teams in each group plus five reserves. In the selected courses there is never any problem because the selection is such, there are precisely two teams with five reserves.

Every course for the past nine years has begun with a testing and measuring programme. It is important with young players to point out particular weaknesses in their fitness levels so that they can go away and improve them. I well remember one player who was a prop, his arm strength was poor. He was told of the importance of strong arms and shoulders for scrummaging and for mauling, and he was given advice on what he should do. The following year he came back and recorded one of the highest arm strengths we have ever measured. In his first year we used a simple press-up test but on his return we used dips on parallel bars because it is a much more valid test. Ian Davies, the player in question, was rather disappointed at first to learn this, as he had worked so hard at press-ups that he could do over 200! As part of the fitness programme we show players the kind of activities which will improve their fitness. Various forms of weight-training and basic conditioning systems are illustrated, as well as how do-it-yourself equipment can be made.

On the first day too we have an assessment period. This consists of a short game and gives coaches the chance to assess the players and adjust their coaching accordingly. Individual Skills Clinics are held each day and attention given to unit and team practice. Extensive use is made of film and there are sessions on the Laws. At the end of the week a match is played and invariably the contrast between this and the assessment game is light-years apart. Players on these courses do not ever doubt the value of coaching.

We have progressed through the lower echelons of the game until we now come to the senior National Team. Wales, of course, revolutionised the approach to international Rugby by, for the first time in 1967, setting up a National Squad of players. Prior to that time international sides assembled on a Thursday and had a "run-out" on Friday. This really was woefully inadequate preparation by any standards. In 1969 I wrote an article on the value of a National Squad. I still think that it summed up attitudes at that time and therefore I make no apology for reproducing it here:

An international Rugby Football game ought to mirror everything that is best in Rugby. The attitude, skill and spirit should be of the highest possible standard. All too frequently this is not the case, the quality of play is sometimes extremely poor and a bad image of the game emerges. It is only the occasion which prevents the match from being a complete travesty. This is particularly unfortunate nowadays when so many international matches are televised, for then Rugby loses the opportunity of selling itself to millions of people. This idea of creating interest in the game is especially meaningful in a society where there are many activities competing for the time of young men.

But why should international players perform badly? Why should international teams serve up unattractive fare? The reasons are complex but the truth lies partly in the fact that a national side although it may be bristling with talented individuals is really a "scratch" team. It is true, too, that the period when the team is together prior to an international match is too near and too short to be able to do anything positive about the way in which the game will be played.

What can be done? It is almost characteristic of the British approach to life in such circumstances to do nothing and, like Mr Micawber, to wait for "something to turn up"! The Welsh Rugby Union has attempted to make a more realistic and positive approach by establishing a national squad of players. The squad, which usually numbers about twenty-five, is chosen on the evidence of the trials and then meets for practice on several occasions during the season. Selection for the national side comes from within the squad but players from outside are also considered. The system obviously has to be flexible and players are added to and taken out of the squad according to the form they display. It is hoped that this method will not only raise the standard of the national side but also the standard of the game in Wales as a whole. The national side is the "shop-window" of Welsh Rugby and from its performance many young players find motivation and inspiration. If only for this reason the national side must be given the opportunity which will enable its players to demonstrate high standards.

The squad system undoubtedly provides this opportunity. The advantages are many, and very high on the list must come the spirit which one is able to create and develop within the group. It really is not quite fair to ask a player to play what, certainly for the new cap, may be the most important game in his life with other players some of whom he may have met the day before for the first time. While it is true to say that the fundamentals of the game are the same at all levels it is incorrect to assume that the tactics too should be the same. Tactics will be influenced by conditions, by the opposition and by the particular players in a side. The squad therefore gets the opportunity of practising the tactics it has decided to employ; of playing to strength and away from weakness. Very few national sides are ever capable of playing without demonstrating certain defects in their play. Through the squad there is a chance of analysing these defects and trying, through practice, to eradicate them. This, in turn, improves the overall team performance. The Welsh Squad is composed in such a way that should a player selected for the national side have to withdraw for any reason, his place is covered and, what is most important of all, covered by one who has been involved in practice. This player can therefore fit into the game without any problem whatsoever.

It will be clearly seen that this approach by the Welsh Rugby Union is the sort of thoughtful preparation which is essential if an international match is to be all that it ought to be. This does not mean to say that the system does not have its critics—indeed they are many, varied and voluble! "Professionalising the game" is the cry. If wanting to get better, raise standards and in doing so attract others to the game is professionalism then the Welsh Rugby Union is guilty. But the view of most people would be that professionalism is making money out of the game and in this respect the Welsh Rugby Union is as jealous as anyone of the amateur nature of Rugby Football. They intend it to remain so but this does not mean that playing standards must stand still, which is what will happen unless positive steps are taken to improve them.

The critics will also say that this establishment by Wales of a national squad is merely a means of ignoring International Board Resolutions relating to the assembly of national sides before a game. This is most definitely not the case. This action by the Welsh Union is concerned with much broader issues. It has committed itself to coaching as a means of improving the game and this must be applied at all levels. Younger players will follow more easily if the same principles are practised by international players. The aim is to develop a Welsh pattern of play and in this respect the squad concept is an investment for the future.

One would argue that the squad system is completely logical and essential in order to raise the standard of the game at national level. One cannot guarantee, however, that it will always produce a game worthy of the occasion but at least it would not be for want of trying.

It would appear that the logicality appealed to other people too, because, in spite of the early out-cry against squads, by the end of 1969 every team that played against the 1969–70 Springboks was based on the squad concept. As far as Wales is concerned there is very little difference in organisation from that which I described in 1969. The National Squad, which now numbers about 30 players, is selected after the Final Trial in January and only meets on the Sunday before each international match. In a season, therefore, we have four National Squad sessions. The team (i.e. 21 players) assembles for the match on a Thursday afternoon when another practice session is held. Opposition, if required, is provided by local Rugby clubs. If the match is away, then the players stay overnight and travel on Friday mornings. For home games the players disperse to their homes after the Thursday practice and reassemble on Friday evening.

The programme for each National Squad session depends of course on what the National XV Coach feels ought to be covered. In general the day will cover discussion on the last game with everyone contributing; an analysis of strengths and weaknesses displayed in the last game, often supported with visual material in the form of a video-tape recording, and a quick look at the game ahead. This is followed by two practical sessions, before and after lunch. In the first practical session, time is taken to concentrate on areas where we felt we did not succeed, while the second session is concerned entirely with the tactical implications of the coming game.

One other feature, too, is that frequently international panel referees are invited to referee for short periods. This has paid dividends in reducing the penalties awarded against us. Players often act in ignorance of the Law and it is much easier to sort out these problems on the practice field rather than wait until the actual match and perhaps pay heavily for your shortcomings. The final match practice on the Thursday merely serves to reinforce and re-emphasise the points mentioned and practised on the previous Sunday. This kind of organisation and thoughtful preparation is essential if quality players are to take the field with confidence and play to their potential.

REFEREES

Let me now look at the position relating to referees. They do not come under the authority of the Coaching/Laws Committee but they do come within my terms of reference, for I am charged with the responsibility for the training of referees. I welcome this, for referees are an integral part of the Rugby structure and failure to make efforts to raise refereeing standards will certainly hold back other attempts to lift technical standards within the game.

The WRU has developed in recent years a system of referee training and grading which extends from beginner through to international level. Beginners attend a course which consists of six two-hour lecture sessions backed up with a whole day's practical work. Those who wish to sit the WRU Referees' Examination must, of necessity, have attended a WRU Referees' Course. The examination is split into two parts. The first is a written paper which is a searching test of knowledge of law. Those who reach the required standard qualify for the second part, which is an oral examination usually lasting about 25 minutes.

When referees are qualified they referee initially at Welsh Districts and Youth level. They are reported on by clubs and the top referees are promoted to the WRU Referees' List, which has an establishment of 130 referees. For the first year they act as probationers, during which time they are reported on by clubs and assessed by WRU observers. If their position is confirmed they enter the List proper and through the grading system in operation can go right to the top of the refereeing tree.

The grading scheme attempts to categorise all those referees on the WRU List. In order to do it in the most effective manner a two-tier system has been adopted. First, each club completes a simple grading card which places the referee according to his performance on a 10-point scale, 0 being poor and 9 excellent. The cards are returned to the Union Office and are coded for computerisation. The computer print-out gives an indication of the ability of the referee. We also have a group of Referee Assessors, former WRU Referees, who, on the evidence of club cards, observe certain referees. In this case, the assessment is a very detailed one, and depending on the results a referee at the end of the season may either be promoted within the grades or indeed removed from the WRU Referees' List. There are five grades:

Grade 1: Exchange level. (Within the Four Home Unions and France there is a scheme where the best referees are "exchanged" on a reciprocal basis. The purpose is to give experience and to try to pick out future International referees.)

Grade 2: Capable of refereeing any WRU game.

Grade 3: Capable of refereeing selected WRU games.

Grade 4: Up to the minimum standard required to remain on the WRU List.

Grade 0: Subject to observation during the season.

No referee may remain in the "0" grade for two consecutive seasons. He must either gain promotion or be removed from the WRU List.

Apart from courses for beginners a tri-annual residential conference is arranged for "List" referees when international panel referees from other Unions are invited to present papers, and one-day conferences are organised for other referees who have not yet attained promotion to the WRU List.

The scheme offers many incentives and in doing so recognises the fact that most referees are very ambitious and want to do well. This must inevitably raise refereeing standards.

PUBLICATIONS AND VISUAL AIDS

Finally, as far as organisation is concerned, let me mention publications and visual aids. These are important back-up areas in any Coaching Scheme. The RFU have a fine record in the publications field. They have produced many books which have made an excellent contribution to the game. Their efforts have made any attempt by the other Home Unions largely superfluous. In fact, as a result of discussions at the annual meeting of coaching representatives from the Four Home Unions and France, it has been agreed to use each other's material and so avoid unnecessary duplication and expense. The result is that we use the RFU's books such as *Better Rugby* and *The Guide to Players*, while the RFU are the biggest customers for the WRU wallcharts entitled "Improve your Rugby Football". Another example is the RFU/WRU joint publication on Mini-Rugby.

Both Unions have extensive film libraries. Such films can be either promotional or instructional or sometimes both. In this latter category comes the WRU's film on Mini-Rugby. It has had fantastic sales throughout the world and was made possible by generous financial aid from Barclays Bank Limited.

The latest "aid" in the coaching field is the video-tape cassette recorder. This kind of sophisticated equipment has an important part to play both in the training of coaches and referees and in the preparation of teams. A word of caution, however; to maximise its use very careful planning is essential and no one should contemplate using equipment of this nature unless time, usually a lot of it, is given to preparation. Used well and wisely it will repay dividends but misunderstood and badly handled it could turn out to be a very damp squib.

COACHING AIDS

Many coaches use a variety of coaching aids. I have found two to be of particular benefit. They are the scrum machine and the tackle bag. I would not pretend that they provide the final answer but they are an "aid" and I use the word correctly. We use these two pieces of equipment at all levels in Welsh Rugby, from coaching beginners to the Welsh National Squad itself. We have found the equipment supplied by John Moore & Son, Dept 1, West End Works, Magor, Gwent to be of excellent value.

SECTION II
Technique, Skill and Method

5 PRINCIPLES OF PLAY

In my early teaching career I can vividly remember how I tried to teach Rugby football to boys in Peterborough, the vast majority of whom had never seen a Rugby match let alone handled a Rugby ball. In the absence of any real guidance I taught the Rugby in the way that I myself had been taught it some 14 years previously. In retrospect it was very unenlightened teaching, but at least I was an enthusiast and that I am sure made up for my many shortcomings. Of course as I gained experience I also gained confidence and I began to question some of the standard practices which had become an accepted part of the Rugby scene. I read avidly all the Rugby literature, but there really was very little on teaching and coaching. I gradually became aware of the need for the Rugby authorities to give much more help in this area of the game. It was this thinking which prompted me to write to Douglas Prentice, then Secretary of the Rugby Football Union— a matter to which I have already referred.

I taught the game in those days by teaching individual basic techniques such as passing, tackling, kicking etc., usually on the basis of one technique per session. It would be an over-simplification to say that I got a group of boys and said, "Today I am going to teach you how to pass, next week, how to tackle; then how to kick, pick up the ball, scrum, line-out, backs in attack and so on. If you do well, just before Christmas we might even play a game!" It was not quite as bad as that but I knew of plenty of schools where the approach was worse. In fact I would go so far as to say that some teachers still persist with this kind of approach in spite of the work which has been done by all the Home Unions in the past ten years. This is largely because there are some people who are not prepared to give up the time to attend courses and so up-date their methods.

What had happened was that when people analysed the game, they saw that in the game there was passing, running, tackling, kicking, rucking, mauling etc., and assumed that in order to teach Rugby football all we had to do was to teach these components. It would be quite wrong to say that it did not work because it did, but it was not the most effective way and it certainly was not the most enjoyable. Players were subjected to long periods of boring practice which had little relevance to the game. We were all eager for guidance and enlightenment but there was not too much of that about, at least until the advent of coaching in the mid-sixties.

Fortunately, there were individuals who in their own schools and colleges (club coaches at this time were unheard of) were challenging a lot of the concepts and producing their own solutions to the problem. One thinks immediately of Ian Beer, Jeff Butterfield, Bob MacEwen, John Robins and Gerwyn Williams. When the Rugby authorities got themselves organised they were able to call upon the expertise of such men.

My opinion was that we were dealing with the "bits and pieces" of the game without ever relating them to the total game. It was a case of the sum of the parts not adding up to the whole. I came to the conclusion that we had to change the concept if we were to produce teaching and coaching patterns which would stand scrutiny in the light of the work which had been done on the acquisition of skill. However, it was not until I became the WRU Coaching Organiser that I was really able to develop these ideas. On my appointment I was able to devote all my energy and thinking to the game without the distractions of having to be concerned with earning my living! Even more important was the fact that I was in a position of great influence because I was directing the Coaching Scheme and as such was responsible for the training of all coaches.

In describing the "bits and pieces" approach I use the analogy of the artist who is asked to paint a large mural. He does not begin by going to fill in little bits of detail. He begins by making a quick outline in chalk so that he can picture what the total project will look like. Everything is in perspective, or at least, if it is not so, he can make very quick alterations. Everything can be related to the whole. We must begin with the whole, in other words we must begin with the game.

I have tried to look at Rugby football and produce what I consider to be the essential principles of play. My thesis is that if we want to play the game well then we must know what the elements are in the 15-a-side game which will ensure that we do just that. These "principles of play" then become the corner-stone of our game and the foundation of our coaching pattern. I want to emphasise that these principles are not original. How could they be, for they have been there for as long as the game has been played. What is original is the way they have been brought together under the heading "principles of play", and used as the basis for a coaching programme. I must say too that this is a purely personal choice, other people may want to disagree or expand the principles which I list. They are, of course, perfectly entitled to do so. One must beware, however, of making things too complicated and too involved. Remember that our motto should be "Success through simplicity".

Let us begin by asking the question, "What does a team have to do when it has possession in order to play well?" In my view it must do three things: go forward, support the ball and keep the ball moving. "What then must a team do when the opposition have the ball?" This can be summed up by stating that the opposition must be subjected to pressure.

These then are my four principles of play:

1. Go forward
2. Support
3. Continuity
4. Pressure

Some people express surprise that "Possession" is not one of my principles. I regard "possession" as an objective and not a principle. Let us examine the thesis in greater detail.

Go forward

No team that does not go forward when it has the ball will ever score a try. This is a simple truism which should be emphasised time and time again. No team can play the game well going backwards or sideways, but many try! The team must be aware of the fact that they can only play well if they go forward and here I would stress the word "team" as opposed to the individuals who comprise it. Attacking the opposition goal line becomes a priority and is much more effective than attacking the touch lines which so many teams seem to do.

This principle amounts to a contract between members of the team. If every player, every unit, tries to go forward then there is some organisation and other players can co-operate because they know what is about to be attempted. It is very difficult to play with those players who decide to opt out and play the game on their own.

Support

If a team in possession of the ball is going forward then the attack can only be sustained if there are players there capable of carrying it on. This is why support is such an important principle of play. It is a fact that no player in any team at any level throughout the whole of the game ever has the ball in his hands for longer than about one minute. Most people are amazed when they are told this, but if you are in any doubt put it to the test at the next match you watch. Select any player and, while the ball is in play, time the number of occasions when he has the ball in his possession. I will guarantee that at the end of the game the total time will not come to more than about one minute.

This in itself poses the next question. If a player only has the ball in his hands for one minute in a game lasting 80, what does he do in the other 79 minutes? The answer is that he supports the ball.

In order to ensure that a team has good support play the coach has to work on three factors: attitude, skill and fitness. A player's attitude to support must be correct. He must *want* to support the ball. There are many players whose work-rate notably falls away as soon as they get rid of the ball. I can think of one player in particular, an international now and a British Lion, who was a dynamic ball-carrier but whose work-rate dropped appreciably when he did not have possession of the ball. However, the Welsh selectors realised his potential and he was drafted into the National Squad. This gave us the opportunity to work on his support play and now because of his willingness to work "off the ball" he makes many more contacts with it.

Willingness to support—and in essence this means to run—is not the only factor. Good support play requires a great deal of skill; reading the game and as a result knowing when, where and how to support the ball-carrier. A simple example will illustrate what I mean. A player could be driving up-field with the ball in his hands, but the support players could be so close that when the ball-carrier is checked they over-run him—no skill in support. Alternatively, in the same situation the ball-carrier could decide to pass, but because of the presence of the opposition in numbers and because of the closeness of the supporters the ball gets tangled up—no skill in support. Players must appreciate the need to support in depth and to adjust their alignment according to the position of the ball-carrier and the opposing players.

Finally, it is obvious that the most positive attitude and a high degree of skill is of little value if the player or players concerned cannot get there. Fitness is therefore a prime factor in support play. One of the great support players of recent years has been Dai Morris of Neath and Wales. He was nicknamed by the Welsh players, "Shadow". This was because Dai was always there. There are those who would argue that support play is the stock-in-trade of the flanker. This is true but all players must be aware of their support roles as soon as they have given up possession of the ball. Barry John, of incomparable skill, was a marvellous support player and scored many tries by suddenly appearing from no-where. Steve Fenwick in the present Welsh XV is another player whose support play is a model for all players.

Continuity

We now have a situation where the team is going forward with support. In order to press home the final advantage it is necessary to keep the ball moving. An unplayable ball can only produce the whistle from the referee and the game stops. The team must then learn to develop continuity, i.e. the means by which the game is kept alive. Running, handling, kicking, rucking, mauling are all continuity skills. Badly performed they can destroy continuity, stop the game and, even worse, often give possession to the opposition.

Continuity is not just a matter of technique and skill, it is also a reflection of attitude. Individuals, units and the team must *want* to keep the ball moving. British Rugby in the past was notorious for its lack of continuity. This was because we were scrum and line-out orientated and as soon as there was a breakdown in play there would be a perceptible relaxation in work-rate and a tacit acceptance that the referee would blow his whistle. The game would stop and be restarted with a scrum. Alternatively, a player would kick the ball into touch and again play would stop to be restarted with a line-out. This is not to say that there are not occasions when it is appropriate to kick to touch, but so often it is a soft option and players must be encouraged to reject soft options.

Pressure

Even the best organised teams know that in normal circumstances ball possession during a game will have to be shared on an almost 50-50 basis with the opposition. Therefore, as well as observing certain principles when we have possession of the ball—viz., go forward, support and continuity—we also need to know what to do when the opposition have the ball.

It is best summed up in the word "pressure". We subject the opposition to "pressure"; we take the game to them; we deny them time to develop attacks; we deny them space in which to move. Pressure causes the other side to make mistakes and mistakes give us the opportunity of regaining possession. Some may say that this is a negative way of playing the game but I would challenge that view. Remember that earlier I defined "positiveness" as *causing* things to happen. Pressure causes mistakes to occur, the negative approach would be to wait for mistakes. Some teams in the absence of pressure can play for long periods without making any mistakes at all. The inference then is obvious, pressure is a fundamental principle which the opposition must be exposed to when they have the ball.

These then are my four principles of play. I am sure if I thought hard enough I could come up with some others but I think they would be superfluous. I base this assessment on the fact that Wales have operated on this basis for the past eight seasons and in terms both of results and quality they have not served us too badly!

My thesis then is, that if in order to play the game well we have to observe certain principles of play, then these are what we should be dealing with in coaching sessions. Individual technique, unit skills and so on are merely the means to an end and that end is: go forward, support, continuity and pressure.

It is my intention to deal in some detail later in this Section with coaching method, but in order that my chapters on the role and function of the forward and back units should be more clearly understood it is necessary for me first to explain two points.

Any coach faced with the task of trying to improve team performance, and working on principles of play as a means to this end, has to decide where the emphasis should be directed in his coaching. He can only do this if he is capable of assessing the role of the individual, the unit and the team. Assessment of this nature can cause problems because the inexperienced coach often cannot "see the wood for the trees". I therefore work on the basis that in any performance be it individual, unit or team there are certain *key factors*. A coach when trying to appraise performance should use the key factors as a kind of check list. For example the key factors in scrummaging are foot positioning, snap shove/lock and mechanics; if something is wrong with a team's scrummaging then the coach initially should look at these three key factors. They provide guidelines on which the coach can work. Perhaps the ball is very slow in coming back—check the foot positions. Key factors may not provide all the answers but at least they eliminate some of the possibilities and frequently prevent entry into a blind alley.

The second point concerns technique and skill. I have referred to them frequently so far, but without defining what I mean by these terms. I have to say immediately that skill psychologists would quarrel with my definition and they would probably be right. However, they do not have to coach coaches. What I am concerned with is that coaches and players understand what I am talking about; if in the strict academic sense my reasoning is not quite "on target" what does it matter?

Technique for me is merely a movement pattern, e.g. passing a Rugby ball from A to B requires technique. The complete tyro can quickly learn to pass the ball with an acceptable technique, in the sense that the ball travels at the right speed, the right height and to the correct place. However, being able to produce this kind of technique in isolation from the game, where there is plenty of time, lots of space, few distractions in terms of other players, in other words a pressure-free environment, is one thing. Reproducing it in the game is a totally different matter. Selecting techniques, performing them under pressure, making decisions as to when and how are the components of skill. Our total concern as coaches must be with the development of skill. This does not mean that we must neglect technique but we must get it in perspective and realise that technique is merely a part of skill. Perhaps I can sum this up by saying as I always do on coaches' courses: "It is more important to teach a player when to do something than it is to teach him how—and much more difficult!"

6 WINNING POSSESSION

The term "QP Factor" was first used in the RFU *Guide to Coaches* (1966); it was a MacEwenism! Bob MacEwen's keen and logical mind produced a few other terms and phrases which have now entered the Rugby vocabulary. QP refers to "quality possession"—some people use the term "good ball" which is just as effective. Some years ago, when these phrases were being bandied about, Colin Meads of New Zealand made the comment that all this business about good and bad ball was a load of nonsense. He said, "As far as I am concerned there is only 'ball' and we want it." It was the kind of simplistic statement which drew a hearty round of applause from those, and there were many at that time, who thought that coaching with its new theories and jargon was a load of rubbish too. However, quality possession was a new concept. It indicated that merely to win possession was not enough; we were seeking the kind of possession which could be used most effectively. The immediate effect of this thinking was to make players aware of the role they had to play. Much more attention was paid to developing the skills which would produce quality ball. The whole idea gendered a new awareness of what was required in order to play positive effective football. The simple facts of Rugby football are that the game begins or ends on the foundation-stones of possession. We must apply ourselves to this as a priority objective and, what is more important, translate it into practical deeds on the field.

British Rugby for years had no real Rugby priorities in the technical sense. We played the game "off the cuff". The game was very dependent on brilliant individual players, usually backs, who occasionally were able to lift international matches from relative mediocrity. However, British Rugby in the pre-war and immediate post-war era was not really exposed to efficient forward play, epitomised by New Zealand and South Africa in particular. In the fifties and sixties there were nine tours, either by New Zealand or South Africa to Britain or by the Lions to those two Countries. It proved one thing: the standard of our forward play was nowhere near good enough to compete on equal terms with the All Blacks and Springboks. A new appraisal was required. Initially, of course, we looked at our forward play, but now I believe we have carried the thinking a few stages further on. There was a period when only the five tight forwards were regarded as ball-winners, the back row were defensive destructive players and backs were those who were expected to score tries—if they could get the ball.

Nowadays when we talk of ball-winners we do not think only of the front five or even the whole pack, we expect backs to be ball-winners too and there are lots of examples in recent international matches of Welsh backs setting up mauls from which we have produced possession and subsequently scored a try. I was careful when naming this Chapter not to call it "forward play". If I had done so I could guarantee that backs would not read it. We have tried to develop a style of play where any player can become a ball-winner and any player a ball-user. The present Welsh international front row, Grahame Price, Bobby Windsor, and Tony (Charley) Faulkner have all scored tries in international matches. Very few, if any, other countries can match that record.

Again, it did not just happen, it is something we had to work for; first by influencing attitudes and then by developing the necessary skills. Of course I cannot deny that it is forwards who are primarily concerned with winning possession, just as it is primarily backs who are concerned with using it. These are their prime functions in set-piece situations. Once the ball is in open play, then we have 15 players not 15 specialists, and every player must be encouraged to perform whatever function is necessary at the time. Without doubt, however, our first task in Wales in the late sixties was to improve our forward play.

I suggested to the WRU Coaching Advisory Committee in 1968 that we should begin to assess Welsh forward play by carrying out a review of the part which the back row played in the British game. I was convinced that the largely negative, defensive role of British back-row players was detrimental to the ball-winning capacity of the forwards, and in any event changes in the laws had drastically limited the movement of the back row. It was significant, however, that very few back-row players had reshaped their game. It was almost entirely the recipe as before, except that the law changes made them even more ineffective than before.

The WRU Advisory Committee took up the challenge and produced the now celebrated paper on *Back-Row Forward Play*. I use the word "celebrated" because in my judgement it revolutionised Welsh International forward play, which in turn had a tremendous influence on British forward play. Through this paper were sown the seeds of the Lions' successes in New Zealand in 1971 and South Africa in 1974. Good though the paper was, great credit must also be given to the WRU Selection Committee at that time, Messrs Harry Bowcott, Cliff Jones, Clive Rowlands, Rees Stephens and Jack Young. They decided to support the Advisory Committee by implementing all the recommendations. Clubs were informed that the National Selectors were no longer looking for open and blind-side wing forwards. They were seeking right and left flankers and players selected for trials or international matches would be expected to play to this pattern. Clive Rowlands who was also Coach to the Welsh XV insisted that players played in this way. Fortunately we were successful and Wales won the Triple Crown in 1969; in fact we only just missed the Grand Slam because we drew with France in Paris 8 points all. I say "fortunately" because such forthright action by the WRU Selectors produced a great deal of controversy. Many people felt that skill was being sacrificed for size. This claim could never be substantiated. In fact, as I have stated earlier, Wales at that time had the lightest back row in international Rugby:

Mervyn Davies (just under 15 stone), John Taylor (13 st 7 lb) and Dai Morris (12 st 12 lb). They played together for five seasons, all of them after the publication of the paper. I remember at the time stating that the paper aims were concerned with "function" rather than "physique". We did one other thing which helped to get the thinking right. We rejected the term "wing forward" and used "flanker" instead, the implication being that the latter had a different role to play. We even changed the names of the positions in our international programmes. Rarely now in Wales do you hear the term "wing forward" certainly not among young players.

I now reproduce the paper in full, because although the past seven or eight years may have changed some of the detail, the basic philosophy and methodology is as sound as ever.

BACK-ROW FORWARD PLAY

In presenting this review of modern back row forward play, we thought it advisable to consider first the usual formation employed by most club and representative sides at the moment.

For many years the accepted formation has consisted of an open and blind-side wing forward, and a No. 8 forward. From set scrum, line-out and in loose play the prime function of the open-side wing forward has been to prevent the opposing outside half making a break. Indeed it has been expected that he will, if worth his salt, completely obliterate the outside half with a series of devastating tackles. In many cases the open-side wing forward pursued this end with such singlemindedness that his whole contribution to the game consisted of a series of hit or miss sorties against the outside half. If successful he disrupted completely the opposition attacks and put the outside half out of the game; if unsuccessful he put himself out of the game.

The blind side was expected to deal with the opposing scrum half. He was expected to harry the scrum half from scrum, line-out, ruck and maul. His contribution was essentially destructive and he was built for this purpose. Usually heavier and less mobile than the open side, who, in his perfected form, was an animal bred for speed, mobility, ferocity and occasionally intelligence.

The No. 8 was expected to prevent the scrum half running near the scrum and to cover across the field behind the three-quarters—in the classical idiom—to corner flag. He was usually the taller and heavier of the three, and because of his position in the scrum was expected to push. He was also often used as a line-out jumper. Unlike the two flank forwards who were never expected to commit themselves to rucks or work generally as tight forwards, there were schools of thought that considered him basically a tight forward and yet others who were happy to see him as an auxiliary flank forward free to run at will and set himself above the donkey work of scrum, line-out, ruck and maul.

This formula of back-row play has developed over recent decades and has been successful at club and representative level in domestic Rugby. We have only needed to reappraise the situation when faced with outstanding scrummaging and rucking sides from overseas.

However, there have been internal factors that have worked against this formation.

The first was the law that prohibited fighting for the loose-head in the scrum, thus virtually assuring possession to the side that put the ball in the scrum. This law whilst increasing the need for predatory wing forwards also gave rise to the realisation that the ball from the ruck was of more value than the ball from the set piece. This realisation put pressure on the back row to arrive first at the point of breakdown and either rekindle or originate an attack.

The second factor was the law that limited the movement of back row forwards until the ball was heeled from the scrum. This made the voracious intentions of the open side in particular much more difficult to indulge.

Another factor was the use of back row as a means of creating attacking opportunities from the tight thus putting an added burden on the back row as a whole.

Finally and probably the farthest reaching in its implications was the realisation that in order to achieve good ball from the ruck it required the active participation of eight forwards. Certain countries have known this for years but the rather misguided arrogance of the Welsh, and their faith in their own undoubted individual brilliance, has obscured the necessity for combined graft to achieve good ball.

The sum total of these factors creates a situation that at least requires us to review the present format, and at most, points irrevocably to the conclusion that our system is wrong.

The policy of any team should be to attack and to do this they require the ball cleanly at the right time; this leads us to the conclusion that the prime consideration of any pack of forwards is to create good ball and this requires the involvement of all eight forwards at scrum, line-out, ruck and maul.

Since the new laws governing the back row have limited the success of the open side in his specialist destructive role, the reasons for his very existence have been eroded. In addition it is virtually impossible for one man to fulfil the duties now ascribed to this specialist. These duties are more effectively performed by the back row as a whole, and this, allied to their involvement in the search for good ball, gives rise to a theory that is not new in conception, only in its application to British Rugby and Welsh Rugby in particular, where perhaps the cult of specialisation has reached its finest definition.

Duties of the Back Row as a Unit—Defence—at the scrum

We must remember at all times that the back row is part of the pack and that the pack is dedicated at all times to providing good ball.

(i) Therefore at a defensive scrum the back row must push to prevent the other side gaining ground and a consequent clean heel, and also to try to slow the opposing heel.

(ii) They must prevent the opposition advancing over the gain line near the scrum by whatever means they choose to achieve this end.

(iii) When the ball is heeled by the opposition they should attempt to harry the half backs by aggressive defence and capitalise on any errors that they force.

(iv) Form a second line of defence when they have failed to achieve their primary objectives. The first line of defence in this context will be the half backs and three-quarters.

Individual Duties of Back Row at Defensive Scrum

We believe in common with coaches from overseas that at a scrum the flank forwards stay down and push until the ball is out. When the ball is heeled by the opposition they should move *forward* to pincer the scrum half. Most flank forwards in Wales move out of the scrum *backwards* before the ball is out and take up a position opposite the opposing half backs, thereby giving themselves time and space to nullify any moves by them. By doing this they put themselves too far away from the opposing half backs to profit from any mistakes they might make, and whilst by their presence they restrict the range of alternatives available to an outside or scrum half, they actually allow the outside half in particular more time to kick or pass. We feel that the flank forwards should move forward. By doing so they can harry the scrum half, and be in position to capitalise upon any errors.

It has been proved that there is no significant time lag in the arrival at the opposing outside half between flank forwards using either method, and there is much to gain by going forward.

In order for this pattern of back row play to be fully effective, then the outside half must be expected to be primarily responsible for tackling or harrying his opposite number at all times. This should not be very difficult because he has usually the speed and mobility and is better positioned to do this than the flank forwards. There have been several notable examples in recent years of crash-tackling outside halves who have made notable contributions to their sides in defence.

As stated earlier we feel that to adhere rigidly to an "open-side" "blind-side" flank formation is outmoded and that it should be replaced by a "left" and "right" formation with both flankers equally adept at the techniques required at various times on either side of the scrum. This shares the work load in defence and attack and enables us to select men who are generally bigger and more fitted to take the rigours of an all-round forward game—as opposed to playing a six- or seven-man pack with a man detailed to mark the outside half at all times. This is a luxury few teams can afford, and that the individual in contemporary Rugby should be comparable to the human appendix—he is there but what does he do?

Therefore when we refer to "blind-" or "open"-side flanker in this context we mean the flanker who happens to find himself on the blind or open side.

Once the ball has been heeled by the opposition the blind-side forward should go forward to take the scrum half. If the scrum half passes "open" he follows the ball across the field, ready to go in for the ball in case of a breakdown. If the scrum half passes blind he then becomes in effect the open side and reacts accordingly. If the ball is taken by one of the opposing back row forwards coming blind in a back row play, he is to take the first man up with the ball and endeavour to stop the attack as far behind the gain line as possible.

The open side also should move forward on to the scrum half, thereby forming a pincer with the blind side. His own scrum half should be first on to the opposing scrum half and in the event of his creating a breakdown both the flank forwards are in a position to profit. Should the scrum half pass open, then he will follow the ball and make the outside half his main objective. He then follows the ball across the field with the thought uppermost in his mind of being first to any breakdown in order to gain the ball for his side.

The No. 8 also pushes until the ball is out. If the opposition use a back-row move he is responsible for the second man in possession, the flanker taking the first. Usually he will break to the side of the scrum opposite to the side of the put-in. He will use his discretion in this but it is a generally accepted principle amongst top class No. 8 forwards. After ascertaining that there is no danger close to the scrum, he also moves across the field and continues to cover close to the ball. He will generally move across field deeper than the flankers, but in a forward direction if possible. Whilst it is a glorious sight to see a wing pulled down by a corner flagging No. 8, or a dangerous punt fielded, these are not his primary duties, and whilst they are certainly listed among his functions he should not spend his time forever running to the corner flag in the hope that one day he will achieve these spectacular feats. Apart from the few world class No. 8s, one can assume that if he does so frequently, he is neglecting something somewhere. He is a tight forward and must do his share in scrum, line-out, ruck and maul.

Duties at an attacking scrum (i.e. on own put-in)

When the ball is put into the scrum by their own side the back row should stay down to give all support in an attempt to gain a clean heel. We favour the 3–4–1 formation which gives many advantages over any other scrum configuration. The flank forwards should pack at an angle on to the prop forwards and endeavour to counter the natural spread of the front row.

On heeling the ball the whole back row must give all their attentions to supporting the backs in attack. The open side in particular should move in as quickly to support his own outside half as he would when attempting to disrupt the opposition: this often requires a conscious mental and physical effort, but it is as important to back up and rekindle attacks as to tackle and destroy.

There are many moves that involve the back row in attack from a scrum, and mainly they are used to engage the opposing back row and set up a platform for a second-phase attack. These will be discussed as a separate entity.

Back Row at a Line-Out (Opposition throw)

The back row at a line-out must of course contest possession, and in order to do this it is usual for the tallest man or best jumper to mark the opposition tallest man, either at No. 6, 7 or 8.

If the opposition gain possession then the last man takes the first man with the ball; this can either be the scrum half or a peeling forward. It is important that he engages the opposition on their side of the gain line before they have made ground.

The remainder of the back row are to engage the second man in possession. This may be another forward peeling or the opposing outside half.

We must remember that at scrum and line-out we expect our own outside half to be primarily responsible for tackling his opposite number.

At a ruck formed from a short throw to the front of the line-out, Nos. 6 and 7 commit themselves actively to the ruck with the last man in the line-out and the scrum half sharing the duties of defence around the ruck.

Back Row in the Loose

Possession from the loose is vital to constructive attacking Rugby, and the back row have a profound effect upon any team's ability to gain good loose possession.

By backing up in attack and dogged covering in defence the flank forwards in particular should be first to arrive at any breakdown that occurs during a game. This being true they are ideally placed to resuscitate an attack or to instigate a counter attack. If they find the ball is free from the tackled man's hands they should attempt to ensure possession for their own side by picking the ball up, and then feed supporting players or make ground themselves. If the forward is tackled in the process of gaining the ball he must attempt to stay on his feet and turn to form a platform on which his supporting pack can build a successful ruck. On arriving other than first man, a back row forward must still commit himself to the ruck since it is only by intelligent total involvement of all eight forwards that consistent good possession is gained from the rucks. A back row forward should be mentally tuned to the attitude that he wants the ball from the ruck for his own side, and not, as is so often the case, more concerned with stopping the other side doing something with the ball once they have won it. All forwards should be obsessed with a craving to satisfy their hunger for possession of the ball, and this applies to all forwards in all circumstances.

An attacking ruck is created when a side has moved the ball over the gain-line either by kicking or running, and have involved the opposition in a ruck into which its own forwards are moving forward. Because they are moving forward from the last play they should arrive "firstest with the mostest", a necessary ingredient for good re-possession. It is vital that the back row, who should be amongst the first to arrive, commit themselves in these circumstances.

A defensive ruck means that a side has been committed to a ruck on the wrong side of the gain line. They have to turn and run backwards to the play and turn again to enter the ruck from the correct side. This means that they are at a disadvantage, and when this happens close to the line a case arises for one man being detailed to assist the half backs in open defence. It can either be the last back row forward back or someone who has been detailed for this specific purpose.

Back Row in Attack from Set Pieces

From all set-piece attacks involving the back row, the objectives have three common factors:

1. To take the ball as far as possible over the gain line;
2. To commit the opposition;
3. To regain possession.

These objectives are common to line-out and set-scrum manoeuvres and can be achieved in a multitude of plays, as evinced by the French at a line-out and South African and All Black teams from set scrums.

The pattern we have outlined in the preceding pages is not new to Rugby football, but it is the formula which we would recommend as being the best in our considered opinion. It has several points to its favour.

First it enables all eight forwards at all times to concern themselves with possession, particularly in the loose where Welsh forwards traditionally have a failing.

It creates an attitude of mind that concerns itself more with obtaining good ball and playing constructive Rugby than with a set of defensively orientated motives.

It spreads the work load in defence equally between the back row and the half backs, with definite tactical advantages, and gives the back row more freedom to engage itself more closely with the rest of the pack in its search for possession.

It also enables us to select men who are equipped physically to meet the demands of total involvement in forward play, since it obviates the necessity to include in the back row at least one man who has the speed and mobility to counteract the agile running of the opposing outside half. Men with these qualities rarely have the additional virtues of strength and height in sufficient quantities to make a significant contribution to the line-out, scrum and loose play.

The fact that we recommend "right" and "left" flank forwards as opposed to "open" and "blind" means that the effort involved in supporting and backing up the three-quarters is also shared, with a consequent raising of efficiency.

Other coaches may have other ideas, and they will all have circumstances peculiar to their own teams which would necessitate an amendment of this formula. However we submit this as a proved and successful basic pattern for your consideration.

The paper achieved its objective, that of producing back-row players with a more positive approach, concerned with winning possession rather than stopping the other side when they had the ball. The whole back row became much tighter in its approach to the game.

I said earlier that winning possession does not begin or end with forwards. Gradually by working on the attitude and skill of backs they can become ball-winners too. Clive Rowlands always said of his superb 1971 Triple Crown and Grand Slam team that John Dawes and Arthur Lewis, both centres, were the best maulers in the side! Possession is contested in three areas of play, scrum, line-out and ruck/maul situation, and I want in the next three chapters to discuss these aspects of play in terms of philosophy and skill.

7 THE SCRUM

In Britain, we believe that the most exciting kind of Rugby football is that where there is an abundance of running and handling. Many coaches and players feel that all that is required is for them to practise this aspect of the game and exhilarating Rugby will follow as a natural consequence. This is far from the truth, for the game can only be played effectively and successfully in this way by creating the right platform.

The scrum is the most important single platform in the game. It makes such physical demands that it affects one's ability in the lines-out, in the rucks and mauls, in supporting attacks and in covering in defence. In other words it affects a team's overall performance. A good scrummaging side will rarely be completely out-played in spite of other inadequacies in the team. What then are the essentials of good scrummaging?

Attitude as in all other facets of the game looms large! Players must believe that good scrummaging is important. They must be prepared to scrummage for the whole game. Many packs begin a game with a rush of enthusiasm and scrummage well for the first 20 minutes, then they lose their concentration and the will to dominate. This is precisely where the side with the right attitude developed through concentrated practice can reap the benefit.

Clive Rowlands, who was then Coach to the Welsh National XV, was convinced at the beginning of the 1969 International campaign that Wales had to improve its scrummaging if we were to do well. We had a new commitment from flankers because they had been told they had to scrummage, and we spent a lot of time in squad sessions working on our scrum. In those days we attempted to "snap shove" on our own ball, and I can remember saying to Brian Price the captain that we had to drive on every single ball. He replied by saying that it was very hard, but I countered by saying that that was what we had to do if we wanted to achieve success. We stuck at it and we did get success. So much so that by the following season the other Home Unions were themselves forced to rethink their ideas on the scrum.

Another matter concerning attitude is the importance placed on winning a strike against the head. The value of tight-head ball has been grossly exaggerated by the media. How often do we hear or read "... lost the scrums 3–nil"? It is of course, a nice tidy statistical exercise but often it is meaningless. It is perfectly possible for the pack that lost the tight-heads to have been pushing the other pack all over the field. I remember one game especially, Wales against England in Cardiff in 1971. Perhaps England on that occasion won the tight-heads, Wales certainly did not because we did not strike on the tight-head throughout the game. Instead we concentrated on an eight-man shove and as a result England were scrummaged out-of-existence. Where is the meaning in the tight-head count now?

It is the quality of ball which counts, and statistics relating to scrum take no account of quality. If a team has the right attitude towards tight-head ball, the hooker will contribute much of the time to an eight-man shove, and consequently opposition ball, which they will nearly always get even when challenged, is often of poor quality. Here is the immediate opportunity to put them under pressure. Some time ago I had been deputed to watch a certain match on television so that I could report back to the Welsh National Squad meeting a week later. I mentioned to Bobby Windsor, the Welsh hooker, that the hooker of the team in which we were most interested struck every single time on the tight-head. "Yes," said Bobby. "He's a selfish so-and-so." It's not exactly how Bobby expressed himself! It does, however, give a very revealing insight as to how players regard each other. Attitude by itself, however, is not enough, it must be allied to fitness and technique. Fitness is adequately covered in Section III so let me deal with technique and skill.

I use the key factors of scrummaging as my template. These are the guidelines which will help any coach to simplify the problems. The key factors are, foot positioning, snap shove/lock and mechanics.

FOOT POSITIONING

The RFU *Guide to Coaches* coined a profound phrase, it was, "Foot positioning is more important than shove." Perhaps it slightly overstated the case but this is often necessary in order to get some kind of reaction. I know that many forwards regarded the view that there were special kinds of foot positions with amazement. No one had ever told them where to put their feet. Coaching consisted of phrases like, "Get your head in and shove". Correct foot positioning is essential if the ball is to be produced cleanly and quickly or even if it is to be held and its release controlled. The main point is that there must be an effective ball channel. Fig. 3 shows the basic foot positions. These, of course, can be modified to suite individual preferences but whatever is done they must still allow a channel down which the ball can be struck.

The loose-head prop is a key figure. The generally accepted foot placing now is for him to pack with his legs apart, his right foot sometimes almost behind the hooker's feet and his left leg usually slightly in advance of his right leg. This provides a solid base from which to operate. The ball, when it is struck, moves back into the scrum between his legs. It should be made clear that no longer is the loose-head prop expected to follow the ball in so that he can assist the hooker. This was a relic of the 3–2–3 scrum but the idea persisted for years. It must be understood that the loose-head prop has probably the most difficult job in the scrum especially on his own put-in. We should not expect him to do it while he is standing on one leg!

The tight-head prop on his own put-in ought to be concerned mainly with resisting shove and transmitting drive, and he must

Foot Positioning

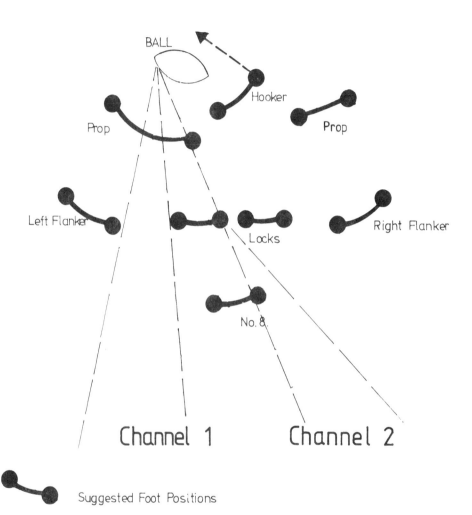

Fig. 3. Basic foot positions and ball channels.

Correct foot positioning is essential for the production of good ball. Channel 1. produces good ball. But it must be struck cleanly and quickly

If the ball is slow in coming then Channel 2. must be used — a good place for the scrum half to pick up the ball, but it is not necessarily good ball.

put his feet in an appropriate position to achieve this end. On the opposition ball his role may be different. If his hooker is attempting to strike for the ball, then the tight-head will be using his outside leg in order to assist the hooker by following in the opposition put-in.

The hooker on his own put-in must first of all be in a comfortable position to strike for the ball. I have long been an advocate of right-foot or far-foot hooking. Apart from the fact that inversion (as opposed to eversion) gives much better control of the ball, the left leg or near foot is mechanically in a much better position to contribute to the strike as well as being able to resist shove and transmit drive. I will say more about the hooker's role later.

Locks must pack in such a way that they do not block the ball channel. This is particularly so for the left-hand lock. I recommend packing with both feet back, although one foot may be slightly in front of the other in order to maintain drive should it be required. The "both feet" back position is much stronger than "one up and one back!"

Flankers and the No. 8 again pack with both feet back, but they must be alive to the fact that they may well have to move their feet in order to control the ball.

There is often a good deal of argument concerning the best ball channel. Reference to Fig. 3 shows that, in essence, there are two ball channels. Channel 1 is the quick one, where the ball is struck down the left-hand side of the scrum through the loose-head prop's legs and between the left-hand lock and the left flanker. Channel 2 is for the controlled heel to the No. 8. Most teams tend to dismiss Channel 1 as being too risky and always aim for Channel 2. This is to deny the excellence of Channel 1, provided the ball is struck cleanly and under control. It demands high standards from both the hooker and the scrum half but the reward can be real quality possession.

If, on the other hand, the ball hits feet and is slow in coming, then Channel 2 must be used in order to protect the scrum half.

Alternatively, the scrum half may be rather slow himself—again Channel 2 ball is required. If a team has a scrum half who is quick and is basically a runner, then a lot of consideration ought to be given to producing Channel 1 ball. Some sides, notably from New Zealand, when they want absolute control or when they want to use the No. 8 in a back-row move, often pack the No. 8 between the left-hand lock and the left flanker. This gives the speed of Channel 1 with some of the safety and control of Channel 2.

I cannot count the number of arguments I have had with that king of scrum halves, Gareth Edwards. He is certainly a Channel 2 man! There are however good reasons why he has this preference. Gareth of course has an enormously long pass, but in order to achieve it he has, like any other scrum half, to "set" himself. If the ball is put in Channel 1 the speed of the service does not allow Gareth time to do this, and he usually has to dive pass or run with the ball. He is such a talented player that, quite frankly, it does not matter where the ball comes, he will nearly always manage to do something quite magical! I believe that we need to give more consideration to the selection of ball channels. When a scrum half break is "on" then Channel 1 should be used, when a long scrum half pass is required then Channel 2 may be the better one. The main point is that we should be thinking about it.

I think it would be appropriate at this stage to say a few more words about the hooker. It is said that hookers have their own private game in the front row, and that match results for them are not decided on points scored but on heads won or lost! If a coach has a hooker with this attitude then he has a job on his hands. It is to convince the hooker what his real function is. As far as the scrum is concerned it is to produce not just ball but quality ball. Many hookers a few years ago persisted in hooking with the near or left foot on their own put-in. Their reason was obvious, they were that much nearer the ball. They argued that if they got the ball back their responsibility was over. This was a view I never could accept, possession does not belong to the individual, it belongs to the team, and it must be the best possible possession so that it can be used effectively. One of my most satisfying moments was persuading an international hooker that he should use his far foot as opposed to his near foot. He changed his technique and in my opinion (and in his) became a better player as a result. One final point is that successful hooking is often the result of a good relationship between scrum half and hooker. Putting the ball into the scrum is quite a difficult task. It needs a great deal of practice but in general terms—the faster the ball is fed, the better the hook will be.

One final point concerning the relationship between scrum half and hooker is the actual timing of the feed. For years the scrum half had always decided when he would put in the ball. Sometimes it went in when the hooker was totally unprepared. Now we have a much more logical situation. The hooker decides. He usually gives a visual signal to the scrum half and this has to be a sounder method.

SNAP SHOVE/LOCK

An explosive drive from seven or eight forwards is difficult to resist but the key word is "explosive". This is why we talk about "snap" shove. It can be achieved by packing down with heads up, legs flexed and being absolutely steady (Fig. 4). It is important to have some word or action to trigger the "snap". When it comes players must drive explosively with the legs and pull in tight with the arms. It is a good idea to get players to shout together when they get the signal. The shout should be "now" or "weight" as is sometimes used in New Zealand. The aim is to ensure good timing of the "snap".

The Welsh pack in 1969 used to "snap shove" on our own put-in and also on the opposition put-in by way of an eight-man shove. However, as other packs got used to what we were doing, they began to copy us and while we were able to try to snap shove on

Fig. 4. The Barbarians *v.* Australia 1975. The Barbarians in hooped jerseys are ready to "snap shove" on Australia's put-in. Note the flexed knees.

the opposition put-in, we were obliged to "lock" the scrummage on our own ball.

The "lock" technique is a very good one, especially if you have a light pack. The Japanese are past masters at locking the scrum, and on their tour of England and Wales in 1973 they were very rarely pushed backwards, if at all, even though they were grossly out-weighted. Players can very easily be taught to lock. The principle is one of the straight line. Try a simple experiment: pick a heavy man, grip his jersey using one hand at chest height. Keep your arm bent at the elbow and ask him to push forward. You will find it extremely difficult to hold him away because your arm will give at the elbow. Now start again but this time lock your elbow straight, now ask him to push. You should hold him off with ease. This is the principle of the lock position: straight back, hips low and straight legs. It is most difficult trying to push an individual who adopts this position.

We now adapt the technique to the scrum. Props obviously cannot get their hips low otherwise there are no pushing points

Fig. 5. The Barbarians *v.* Australia 1975. This is almost a very good lock by Australia on their own put-in. Note, however, how the left lock has completely dropped his hips and how consequently the No. 8 has ridden over his back.

for locks or flankers. They have to modify the position, as do locks to a lesser extent. The No. 8 and the flankers can get in extreme lock positions and be very effective (Fig. 5).

One further development is to lock and drive. The scrum is locked, the ball hooked and held at No. 8. If an eight-man shove has been attempted but the locking pack can contain it, there will be an inevitable relaxation. The locking pack can feel this and it is their signal to drive. Mervyn Davies was an excellent judge of when to hold and drive.

MECHANICS

A look at Fig. 6 will clarify the mechanics of the 3–4–1 scrum. Briefly they are these: the props shove straight forward; the hooker has no shoving responsibility at least on his own ball. However, there is a view now being expressed that the hooker can and should make a shoving contribution on his own ball, not

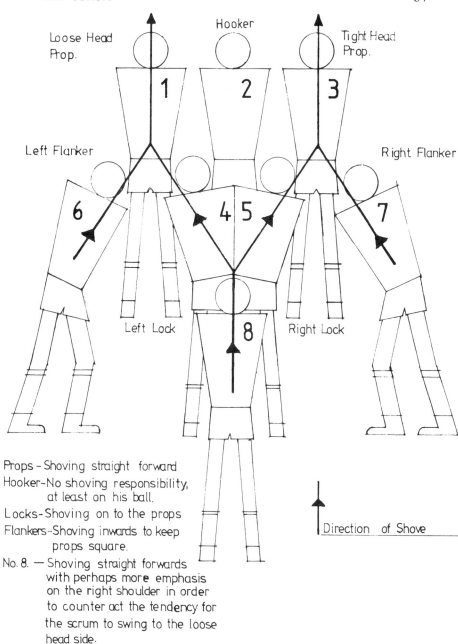

Props – Shoving straight forward
Hooker – No shoving responsibility, at least on his ball.
Locks – Shoving on to the props
Flankers – Shoving inwards to keep props square.
No. 8. — Shoving straight forwards with perhaps more emphasis on the right shoulder in order to counter act the tendency for the scrum to swing to the loose head side.

Direction of Shove

Fig. 6.

necessarily at the moment of strike, but he should be aware of the possibility. The locks shove on the props—obviously the hooker, because he needs to be mobile and free, cannot transmit shove from locks and they must, therefore, concentrate their weight on to the props. Flankers must pack at an angle and shove in on the props in order to keep them square. One cannot overestimate the contribution the flanker can make to good scrummaging—ask any prop! The No. 8 shoves straight, with perhaps more emphasis on the right shoulder in order to counteract the tendency for the scrum to swing to the loose-head side.

Perhaps one of the biggest problems in recent seasons has been the wheeled or screwed scrum. This is a technique calculated to spoil possession. Let us assume that pack A heel the ball, pack B have tried to "eight-man" them but pack A's lock position is so good that they cannot be moved. Pack B no longer try to drive but they screw the scrum viciously around to the left. It will certainly put pack A under pressure and threaten their ball. It is a difficult movement to stop. My colleague Malcolm Lewis has been experimenting with a 3–3–2 scrum, where the left flanker packs along-side the No. 8 and between the right-hand lock and the right flanker. It is too early to say how successful the move will be. The problem, as I see it, is that it takes support away from the loose-head who needs all he can get, and it will certainly expose the scrum half if the ball is not struck to Channel 2. It is worth a try. But perhaps there is a simpler answer. Forwards can prevent a wheel if they know it is coming. The opposition often mix up 8 man efforts with wheels and therefore forwards are not aware what is happening. The other players, however, can see and it is fairly easy to predict by the body positions they adopt whether a team is going to drive or wheel. Perhaps therefore the scrum half should watch and inform his forwards by means of a code-word what is about to happen. This also is worth a try.

Back, however, to the mechanics of good scrummaging. There are some other important principles apart from the obvious ones like low packing, straight backs, flexed/straight legs depending on whether you are going for a shove or lock. I am referring to hands, knees and the position of shoving shoulders.

The importance of grip cannot be overemphasised. It can be clearly illustrated by asking two packs to scrum down, then getting one side to grip really tightly—the effect on the other side is quite remarkable. In the Welsh National Squad we give a great deal of emphasis to gripping in our scrummaging sessions, so much so that Alan Martin has often said to me at the end of the session that his wrists and forearms ache with the effort.

The use of the knees can be combined with that of grip. This applies when you are trying to drive and have bent knees. On the word "ready" you grip tight and push your knees just three inches towards the ground. You immediately put the opposition in a mechanically poor position. Dropping the knees causes the shoulders to move down too, but in the case of the opposition the hips stay put. They therefore have hips higher than shoulders and that is a weak position. If the opposition drop their knees at the same time, then you are in the same relative position as when you started. Try it and see if it works.

Many potentially good scrums fail because the shoving shoulders are in the wrong place. It is useless pushing them into the fleshy part of the buttock. When real force is applied the shoulders will ride over on to the back and the shove is lost. The correct place is immediately below the buttock, and this can easily be found by packing low on the thigh and allowing the shoulder to slide upwards. When it stops this is the right place—nature's niche made for Rugby forwards to shove against.

There has been some controversy over the correct binding for the locks. Most of them now bind with the outside arm through the prop's legs. I was never a great advocate of this method of binding, but I must bow to the superior experience of many international locks with whom I have discussed the matter. I accept that it is easier for the lock and it does leave a clear area for the flanker's shoving shoulder. I have lingering doubts about its mechanical efficiency, but I accept the view of players who have also thought deeply about it and who have proved their theories on the field of play. For those using this technique it is important that the outside arm does not just bind around the thigh. It must come high and grip the top of the prop's shorts. The binding of locks on each other is just as important. I recommend binding on to the top of shorts of the opposite lock. This gives a much stronger position than merely binding around the back and gripping on the jersey.

The emphasis in this chapter has been on the collective contribution of the whole pack and it is right that this should be so. It would, therefore, be unfortunate to start stressing the role of particular individuals. Players often ask me for advice, sometimes I can help them, sometimes I cannot. In the latter cases I always refer them to experienced players whose judgement I respect. It is amazing how much one player can learn from another.

Finally, in the past two seasons there has been an increasing tendency for scrums to collapse, and in many cases it is deliberate. I do not wish to remind players that the deliberate scrummage collapse is against the Law, and that a penalty kick is a futile gesture against the possibility of a broken neck. All of us in Rugby, be we administrators, coaches, referees or players must recognise that any collapsed scrum can cause irreparable damage: players now lying paralysed in hospital are ample testimony. That a player can be so injured in an accident is most unfortunate. That it should be as a result of a deliberate act is unforgivable. We must all act to eliminate such behaviour in the game.

In recent years the line-out has certainly come under fire, but we should not think that this is something new. More than 25 years ago Danie Craven of South Africa, who has made such a marvellous contribution to the game, wrote an outstanding book on Rugby. In it he referred to the line-out as the "illegal child of Rugby". So dissatisfaction with the laws and the way in which the line-out is played is nothing new.

There are those, of course, who advocate that the situation is so bad that the line-out should be abolished. No less a person than Lord Wakefield of Kendal has long campaigned for the abolition of the line-out. He would like to see it replaced with something like a soccer throw-in. The ball, however, would have to be thrown behind a line drawn from the thrower and at right angles to the touch-line.

I must confess that I am not one who would support this kind of change. The line-out is a unique feature of Rugby Union Football and all of us need to work hard to make it function properly. By "us" I mean, in particular, players, coaches and referees, especially referees. I have always been consistent in placing the responsibility for any deterioration in line-out play fairly and squarely on the shoulders of referees. Some people say that I am being unjust but many others, including referees, agree completely with me. In Britain the trouble really began in the post-1971 Lions period. Before that time the line-out was reasonably fair and respectable, at least in Great Britain. I recollect Paddy D'Arcy of Ireland refereeing the 1967 All Blacks in one of the very early games of the tour. He punished them severely in the line-out and as a result was not invited to referee another match, although he was regarded as one of the outstanding officials in the

Fig. 7. Neatly spaced for the throw-in . . .

Four Home Unions at that time. In fairness to the All Blacks, they could hardly be expected to select someone to referee one of their international matches who penalised severely those things which in New Zealand went unpunished.

The Lions went to New Zealand in 1971 determined to do well, and prepare to accept New Zealand referees and their interpretations at face value. The result was a shambles, at least by our standards. It would not have been so bad if it had been confined to

Fig. 8. but then look what happens.

New Zealand, but due to television exposure the "New Zealand line-out" became the norm. The 1971 Lions came back and practised the same techniques. Our referees allowed themselves to be dominated by the new thinking, influenced no doubt by the Lions' success in New Zealand, and within two years the situation was so bad that the International Board had to intervene and made some drastic modification to the line-out laws.

Here was the golden opportunity for referees to establish a new code of conduct, but unfortunately this they singularly failed to do. The line-out is better, but only marginally. Coaches and players in 1973 were prepared to accept the new laws but, because they were not enforced by referees, they slipped into the old routine. I do not believe that we can blame the players, they have to play the game according to the standards which the referee sets—there is no alternative. We in Wales felt that we had to do some rethinking, not in terms of Law but rather in terms of technique and skill. The matter was discussed at Coaching Advisory Committee level and in 1975 we produced a paper on *Line-out Play*. It says all that is needed to be said about the line-out and I therefore reproduce it without further comment.

The changes in the line-out laws which came about in 1973 produced, during the ensuing season, a welter of ill-informed and unintelligent criticism. What most people did not appreciate was that the "new" laws required some rethinking on behalf of coaches, players and referees. The changes were radical enough to require a period of re-adjustment; players in particular had to be convinced of the need to change techniques.

The popular game of the time was to try to devise yet another set of line-out laws. One of our national newspapers even had a line-out law competition! All this vacillation only served to produce uncertainty in the minds of players and coaches. The result is that they have played the line-out rather with the view that it was going to change anyway, so why spend time trying to develop techniques which would soon be outmoded.

We must accept the fact that the present laws with minor modifications will be with us for some time and *we must direct our efforts into developing skill rather than looking for alter-*

natives. This paper, in looking at line-out play, does precisely that.

The line-out should receive as much attention as scrummaging did a few years ago. This emphasis on the scrum certainly improved play and therefore, by the same token, we should be seeking similar improvement in the line-out. There should be just as much pride in good line-out play as there is in good scrummaging. Much is spoken and written when forwards are beaten in the scrums and "heads" are lost. Pride is severely dented. The same should apply if lines-out are lost. To lose a line-out should be as bad as losing a tight head. Superiority in the set-piece will breed the confidence necessary to achieve team success. Quality line-out ball would give backs that extra space and time and consequently they would be under less pressure. These factors should produce a higher standard of back play.

The purpose of the line-out, like the scrum, is to get the ball back into play. It is a means of restarting the game, and a team's objective should be to secure quality ball so that at best, a try is scored or at worst, ground is gained.

Under the new Laws there are enough options for the side throwing in to expect—even guarantee—to win 90 per cent of its own ball.

There are four key factors affecting line-out play which coaches and players should look at:

(1) Throw-In (2) Catch/Deflection (3) Support (4) Variation

1. Throw-In

Throwing-in is the least practised skill in the game today, and therefore there is a considerable lack of quality throwers. Yet, *this is the most important aspect of the line-out.* Without a good thrower, the line-out cannot operate as one would wish it. Everything is so dependent upon how well the ball is thrown in that a large proportion of line-out practice must be given to this skill. A team can have the best jumpers in the world but if the

throw is bad, then their skill is nullified. So often has a jumper
been blamed for poor line-out possession when it was really the
thrower's fault.

Throwers therefore, must have as much a pride in throwing
well as hookers have in hooking, perhaps more so, since on
average there are more lines-out than scrums in a game. It
could be argued therefore that a player should be worth his
place in the team for his throwing ability alone.

Methods   There are two recommended ways of throwing in,
even for young players, but the torpedo throw is the best
method, since it allows greater variation. Alternatively, the
overarm (New Zealand type) or bowling action can be used,
but variation is limited, particularly for a short throw; that is
one reason why New Zealand throw most balls to the middle or
end of the line-out. The most important factor must be accuracy. To develop this a well shaped ball, and, for schoolboys,
one the correct size must be used. Too often in the past a poor
ball has been used for practice. It is wrong to expect throwers
and jumpers to practise with a bad ball and on Saturday to
perform well. During wet conditions also, the ball can be
difficult to grip and so some resin in the pocket may be useful.
Throwers therefore must master the technique of throwing,
practise regularly and so become extremely skilful.

There are many types of throw, from low hard flat throw to
the high slow lobbed one, which should be practised in conjunction with the jumpers, concentrating on speed and accuracy. The thrower will then acquire a certain technique which
will be extremely beneficial to the jumper. He will decide, in
conjunction with his jumper, how the ball is to be thrown in
and this communication and timing will breed the consistency
that is sought.

Selection   Since the advent of the hooker throwing in instead
of the wing, most clubs have thought that he was the only

player to throw in. The first priority is for a person who can throw; who has the suppleness in the shoulder and finds throwing easy. If a thrower cannot be found then obviously someone has to be taught.

Throwers should come from wing, hooker, prop or flanker because this allows for the greatest flexibility. However, if the wing does not throw in, then this releases him to involve himself more in attack and defence, but not enough attention is given to the role of the wing in this situation. Sadly, he often stands idly by. Usually the flankers, hooker or props are not the primary jumpers and therefore one of these would be ideal. The advantages of a forward throwing in are that (i) he operates on both sides of the field, (ii) it releases the wing to be involved in attack and defence, (iii) the backs can perform as a unit, (iv) there may be a more sympathetic understanding towards his fellow forwards. However, to emphasise the importance—the best thrower to suit the team is *priority number one.*

2. Catch/Deflection

Providing the throw is good, then jumpers have a tremendous opportunity to display their skills under the present laws. Most teams would be more than satisfied with three specialist jumpers, but ought to remember that every line-out player is a potential ball winner.

Positioning   The team positions in which these specialists are selected, e.g. lock, No. 8, are not important in relation to their positions in the line-out. It seems the done thing for them is to stand at No. 2, 4 and 6 or 7 with very little variation except perhaps, when a short line is called. More thought must be given to the positioning of these players. For example, positions adopted could be 1–2–3, 1–2–8, 4–5–7 etc. This gives more options to the attacking side and makes the opposing team's task so much more difficult.

Methods of Gaining Possession   Without doubt, the caught ball is the most effective way of controlling possession. The team who has caught the ball have many more options to feed, to drive, to ruck, to maul etc., and the opposition has to be more aware of the offside lines.

Fig. 9. Well caught in the line-out.

In recent years, the deflection/tap has become the norm. In our view, it should be used as a variation and so much more sparingly. A good deflection is a surprise—quicker and requires great skill—but a bad deflection loses ground and probably possession. Opponents who are uncertain whether the ball will be caught or deflected will certainly have problems.

The specialist jumper's attitude must be one of aggression and acceptance of physical contact. He must have pride and *want* to win the ball. This involves regular practice with the thrower, since timing aids winning quality ball. He will discover and develop different techniques of catching, e.g. inside hand leading; high above the head and turning; low to the shoulder and deflecting (one-hand, two-hand, high, low) etc.

Practice   These techniques must then be put under the constant pressure of regular lengthy practice (five minutes will not do) and against increasing opposition to develop skill. Remember the combination of thrower/jumper is as important if not more important than scrum half/hooker.

Upper body suppleness and strength is very important to a line-out jumper and therefore, specific exercises on weights etc., will prove beneficial. However, the most valuable asset is *leg power*, i.e. applying force at speed. A jumper should be able to make a standing jump of 23–25 inches. With specific training with weights, it has been shown that this can improve by as much as nine inches. That is the equivalent of adding nearly three feet to a person's stretch height—a tremendous advantage. It has also been proved that with a step prior to jumping (permissible under the Laws) one can go even higher. Therefore, jumping ability is a combination of handling skill and leg power. This will undoubtedly breed *confidence* and a line-out player of quality.

3. Support

Every player other than the jumper is a support player, including the thrower, since after throwing he should be prepared to adopt whichever supporting role is needed.

The main function of a supporting player is to protect the ball and so ensure his side keeps possession. There are two different roles he may be called upon to occupy, dependent upon his position in the line-out: (a) as a primary supporter (b) as a secondary supporter.

The primary supporters are those immediately next to the jumper. As soon as the ball is touched, they should bind on the jumper, facing the opposition, thus closing the gaps in front and behind. All other players in the line are secondary supporters and should also compress together, and if the ball is caught should attempt to drive as in a maul.

Every player should support aggressively and be alert for any mistakes. There is always an element of risk, especially

Fig. 10. Good support for the catcher.

from a deflection, and supporters must be prepared to react to become ball winners, in particular the thrower and last man in the line-out. Timing therefore is crucial to maintaining possession and so practice with the jumpers is essential. Jumpers too will vary in their method of gaining possession. For example, a player taking a step forward will automatically increase the gap behind him and close the gap in front of him, therefore the timing of the binding for the two supporters will be very different. But the intention is the same, to react quickly, to protect the ball and to ensure possession.

This sort of static support, as it were, in practice sessions, can be very boring and appear unimportant but it is vital to quality possession—ask any jumper. One of a coach's duties is to make each practice session interesting and meaningful.

Plenty of variations of lines-out around the field where supporters have to think differently and work continuously with not
too much talk, will ensure this. Meaningful activity is so important to success.

4. Variety

With the Laws as they stand, there are many tactical variations possible. It is depressing to see continually in club Rugby,
the line-out appearing to be ill-conceived and ill-executed.
From the large number of options available, a team should be
able to select the ones which suit the personnel in that team;
which guarantees the highest possible percentage of successful
quality ball. This calls for a tactical appreciation of each game
by the jumpers, pack leader and captain, to be communicated
to the rest of the team. The jumpers have certain skills and
when these are integrated within the context of the team, these
combined are the options available. The following are examples
which affect line-out variation:

(a) *Type and length of throw* to coincide with a team's skills,
    e.g. high, low, lobbed, flat, hard, soft, long, medium,
    short and feint.
(b) *Length of line-out* (taking into consideration the 15-
    metre line)—long, medium, short and so making use of
    large gaps somewhere in the line out.
(c) *Number of players* in a line-out (any number possible
    from two to eight). The advantages to be gained from a
    shortened line-out are that it (i) suits the skills of the
    team (ii) causes immediate problems to the opponents
    and (iii) it allows the referee to see line-out infringements
    more easily.
(d) *Type of player used*, i.e. specialist and/or non-specialist,
    including the scrum half and positioning of these players
    as mentioned above.

(e) *Use of Backs* These are used in two ways: (i) directly—for a ball thrown over the line-out into midfield for a back to run on to; (ii) indirectly—immediately brought into play after a particular ploy, e.g. directly from a maul/ruck.

(f) *Time and Place of line-out*—when and where on the field should this variation take place. Usually options are used when the side in possession are attacking (in a safety zone), i.e. inside the opponent's half. But good line-out play breeds confidence and options can be used anywhere. However, the jumpers and pack leader in particular must be able to read the state of the game and choose wisely, instead of taking pot luck.

The peel can also be regarded as a variation, although it is probably more widely used than any other. It has specific Laws of its own and these must be observed (Law 23B (13)). The primary objective of the peel is to gain ground by going forward, and therefore the positioning and support of players is crucial. The positioning in the line-out of the player receiving

Fig. 11. Tapping for the line-out peel.

the ball from the jumper and the support he receives is vital to the success of the move. For example, assuming a peel round the back, the best position for this player is No. 2 for he can time his run far better and be supported easily by No. 1. A peel around the front is used far less but has immense possibilities, the most important aspect being that the throw will

Fig. 12. The peeling forward catches the ball and has good support.

probably be more accurate and therefore the percentage of success greater.

Support for the jumper should be just as tight in case he decides to catch the ball, but the timing of the secondary support perhaps is more crucial in order to go forward and maintain continuity. Timing between thrower/jumper and jumper/supporters is vital and calls for good communication, understanding of principles and total involvement which can only be achieved by practice.

Quick Throw

Although a quick throw-in is not a line-out, reference must be made here since it does concern the ball being brought back into play from touch. A team should be alert for the possibility of taking a quick throw-in and thus ensuring possession. This requires a quick decision by the individual and spontaneous reaction by his team. It is disappointing to see this sort of opportunity missed many times in a season as possession is 100 per cent guaranteed. The Law 23B (10) only requires that the ball that went into touch is used, that it has been handled only by players and that it is thrown in correctly. A player could throw it to himself, provided it travels straight and at least five yards.

Defence

Everything that has so far been written has been concerned with the throwing-in team; however it must never be forgotten that the line-out is a chance to contest the ball, and the uncertainty of possession helps make Rugby Football the exciting game it is. Assuming the opposition has won the ball or is expected to win the ball, what then is the role of the defending side?

Defence, like attack, is an attitude of mind; a positive attitude, whereby the object is to regain possession of the ball. Again, this calls for a tactical appreciation of the opposition and therefore continual concentration is essential. This means analysing the opposing team's individual strengths and weaknesses and acting accordingly.

Defensive tactics revolve around three aspects (a) the jumper (b) the primary defenders (c) the secondary defenders.

   (a) The jumper's responsibility is simply to try and out-think and out-jump his opposite number by fair means. He has to decide whether the ball is going to be thrown near him so this needs concentration. If so, he may try to out-jump his opponent by standing (i) alongside (ii) in front (iii) behind. To succeed should be like winning a "ball against the head". Think too of the effect the lost ball has on the beaten opposition jumper.

(b) The primary defenders are those nearest to where the ball is thrown into the line on either side of their own jumper. Because they are nearest the ball, their main responsibility is to stop opposition (i) getting the ball away (ii) regaining possession. They can do this by being the first to close the gaps, getting a hand on the ball, dispossessing, turning the jumper (very effective) or driving.

(c) The secondary defenders are all the other players, including the backs should the ball be thrown into midfield. They have to be alert for the loose ball, the peel, variations and to help drive in case of a catch. The last man in the line-out should be the quickest flanker. The first man in the line-out and the non-thrower should as far as possible remain detached. Their responsibility is to guard the blind side and No. 1 should pressurise the opposition scrum half.

Defence is exerting pressure collectively where it is most needed. It requires concentration and organisation and this is achieved through thought and activity in practice sessions.

Finally, quality line-out play is dependent on having coaches whose aim should be to organise their coaching sessions in the most effective way, players with dedication and pride in improving their skill and referees who will establish a code of conduct which will allow these skills to flourish.

Earlier I referred to the fact that British Rugby for years had been scrum and line-out orientated. The ball was moved to the backs from these set pieces and the hope was that there would be a break and consequently a score. If that did not happen, which was the usual case, then no one bothered too much because the referee would blow his whistle and there would be another scrum or line-out. There was, in other words, no real urgency about our play. Then came Brian Lochore's 1967 All Blacks under Manager Charlie Saxton and Coach Fred Allen, two men dedicated to total 15-man Rugby.

The 1967 All Blacks played some of the best Rugby we had seen in Britain for many years. Like any All Black side they had a superb pack of forwards and very good backs. They were also a tremendous rucking side. New Zealand's particular contribution to the game has been the ruck. This technique originated in Otago and in particular at the University of Otago in Dunedin. In the twenties there was a coach there called Vic Kavanagh, and his son, also called Vic, became one of Rugby's most respected coaches and thinkers on the game. They were known as "Old Vic" and "Young Vic". University packs are usually lacking in weight but they make up for this with their mobility. Old Vic hit on the idea of getting his light mobile pack to form a scrum in loose play. He argued that a group of forwards binding together and driving would be a most effective force despite lack of size. His forwards would hit the opposition at speed and drive over the man and ball. Inevitably the ball would be left for his team to use. This then was the origin of the ruck.

In Britain we called it the "loose scrum" and it was defined as such in the Laws. In the 1966 *Guide to Coaches* we argued that "loose scrum" was a totally inappropriate term because "loose" was the worst possible description for what a team was trying to achieve. If terminology breeds attitude then "ruck" was the term to be used. It was, Bob MacEwen informed us, "onomatopoeic"! We also persuaded the International Board that it was confusing to have two definitions for the scrum, one for the set scrum and one for the loose scrum. The law was changed so that now we have scrum defined and ruck defined—progress indeed.

By the time the tour of the 1967 All Blacks had ended the whole of Britain had gone "ruck" mad. There was also another term being thrown around, that of "second-phase possession". Then we began to hear of "third" and "fourth phase". I have never felt attracted to the concept of "phase football". It is so easily misunderstood. Players begin to play by numbers, "now we will have first phase", and so on. I think my "continuity" concept is a much better way of describing to players what you seek to achieve.

The preoccupation with the ruck got matters out of proportion. People began to get their Rugby priorities in the wrong order. No one denies that the ball won in the loose is a very valuable one, but you have to set up the loose play first. You cannot do that properly unless you win good set-piece ball. Furthermore, having won the loose ball you must use it effectively. The success which the 1967 All Blacks had with the ruck eventually had in my opinion an adverse effect on the All Black game. They too got their priorities wrong, so much so that when I went to New Zealand in 1970 as a Churchill Fellow I found that flank forwards were being played as props because of their mobility and rucking potential. It took the 1971 Lions to expose this kind of thinking.

If New Zealand gave the ruck to Rugby then Wales contributed the maul. This is a relatively new development in the game. It can be traced to a crucial change of law. In 1964 there were some major fundamental law changes. The scrum and ruck off-side lines were created, but the off-side Laws relating to ruck and maul were different. In a ruck the off-side lines were those drawn through the

hindmost foot on each side of the ruck, in a maul the off-side line
was the line of the ball. This difference was a major factor on how
the game was played. For instance, in a maul if the ball was being
moved by hand backwards in the maul, opposition players operating outside the maul could move with it. As long as they kept
behind the ball they were on-side, and when the ball did emerge
they were in a position to make matters uncomfortable for the
scrum half. This demanded that every maul should be turned into
a ruck. The ball would be pushed to the ground, the maul then
became a ruck and different off-side lines came into operation.
Any "fringers" then had either to join the ruck from behind the
ball or retire behind the ruck off-side line.

Once again the International Board acted, they equated ruck
and maul as far as off-side was concerned. In a maul the line of the
ball no longer was the off-side line. Maul became the same as
ruck, i.e. the off-side lines were the hindmost foot on each side of
the maul and no player was allowed between these two lines. For
most people this was merely a change of law, but I saw much
deeper implications as far as the game was concerned. It meant
that it was not now necessary to turn the maul into a ruck. I also
argued that by mauling, a team would have more control of the
ball because it was in the hands. At first I did not impress too
many people because they were still heady with the rucking of the
1967 All Blacks, but of course, as I have already stated I was in
an influential position because I directed the WRU Coaching
Scheme. I took my new theories to New Zealand in 1970 and
even got one or two people to accept them. By my return I had
made up my mind and stated unequivocally that the maul was
more important than the ruck. The result was that Wales began to
maul from choice and ruck from necessity. Both techniques are
obviously important and teams should be capable of performing
both according to the needs of the moment.

New ideas often require new techniques, and we began in
Wales to perfect a mauling technique which was soon taken up by
other countries. Prior to this time the accepted method was to join

the group of players forming the maul and use the hands and arms to try to secure possession of the ball. Other than turning the opposition, if they had the ball, there was no accepted technique. This fact is borne out in some films which the RFU Coaching Advisory Panel made in 1966. I was a member of the Panel at that time and the film on ruck and maul showed no stylised method of mauling. By 1970, however, we had produced a very definite technique which has now become widely accepted.

The key factors in ruck and maul are precisely the same, although of course the techniques are different. The key factors then are:

1. Support
2. Body position
3. Drive
4. Attitude

Let me deal with these principles first before I discuss specific techniques.

SUPPORT

It is impossible to ruck/maul unless you have a sufficient number of players present. Someone coined the phrase "Firstest with the mostest". It is most apt in the ruck/maul situation. Remember, too, that rucking/mauling is not merely the prerogative of the forwards. Many a ball has been lost because a player "departmentalised" himself and said, "That's not my job." Players must learn to read the game and use their judgement in deciding what decision must be made. It may be necessary for a back to set up a ruck/maul or commit himself to one. By the same token it is no use a forward just blindly dashing into a ruck/maul. He may be better employed doing something else.

BODY POSITION

All players should be aware of the fact that the ruck/maul starts at least five yards from where the ball is. The aim is to drive forward, and in order to do this it is essential to get into a low driving position. This is a strong position and enables players to hit the ruck/maul with their shoulders. Try this experiment: make a big man stand upright and get a small player to stand in front of him and place his hand on his chest. Now tell the big player without moving his feet to push his opponent backwards. He cannot do it and this shows the folly of arriving at a ruck/maul in an upright position. You ruck/maul with your shoulders and unless you get them low, the ruck/maul will never move forward.

DRIVE

Originally I used the term "Stay on your feet", but I discarded it because I realised it was possible to stay on your feet without moving forward! I now use "Drive" as a key factor because this ensures that not only do players stay on their feet but they move forward too. So many players get to the ruck/maul and relax, thinking "I have made it". They must be encouraged to work as soon as they get there, otherwise they will never get the ball.

ATTITUDE

Quite simply it can be summed up in the phrase "Ball not the whistle". Every player in the ruck/maul must want and work to produce the ball. Unless we work hard the referee will blow his whistle and we will have to recontest the ball. My good friend Don Rutherford, who is my RFU counterpart, considers that every ruck/maul should be regarded as a failure. I understand his logic but I do not agree with it. Rucks/mauls are a means of maintaining continuity in the same way that handling and kicking are. What I try to get over to players is that, if we set up a ruck/maul but do not win the ball, then that is a failure. I think there is a subtle difference between the two approaches.

I now intend to examine the specific techniques for ruck and maul. As I think it more important, I will take the maul first.

The key man is the ball-carrier. He must try to drive through tackles using his shoulder and screening the ball. This will enable supporting players to take the ball and continue to drive forward.

Fig. 13. A good example of dropping the shoulder and driving.

If the ball-carrier is checked before he can get rid of the ball then he has to create a platform for the maul. He does this by turning and by getting his body in a low, strong, balanced position which will provide a base for the supporting players (Fig. 14). The first two players must bind in over the back of the ball-carrier. They must drive forward and parallel to the touch lines. By coming in this way they seal off the ball from the opposition and in doing so protect possession which must be a first priority.

The next player who comes in must go for the ball so that it can be moved from the middle to the edge of the maul and further away from the opposition (Fig. 15). Other players coming to join the maul must come in from behind the ball. Again they must be in a low driving position parallel to the touch lines. They should also ensure that the ball-channel is kept clear. The ball should now

Fig. 14. The maul platform.

be safe from the opposition and can be fed at the appropriate moment.

There are other methods which are advocated. Some coaches say that the ball-carrier should never turn, that he should continue

Fig. 15. Rip the ball away and move it towards the back of the maul.

to drive forward and push the ball back on his hip holding it there with one hand. Such a player is certainly in a good driving position but the ball is vulnerable because the player has so little control over it. I am convinced that the "turning" technique is much safer and provides a better base on which to establish the maul. There is one danger, and that is that some players turn before they make contact: this is something which needs to be watched carefully for it can reduce the momentum of the drive.

Recently another version of the maul has developed. It is sometimes known as the "English" maul because that is where it originated. Basically it is the same as the maul I have already described except that when the ball-carrier has turned, the first man up takes the ball and then the next two players bind on him. The justification for this technique is that you should secure the ball first and then seal off the opposition. Personally I do not see enough difference in the technique to argue about, at least to any great extent. I still feel that the Welsh technique is sounder. There is no question as to its legality: it effectively blocks off the opposition and prevents them coming through with the ball which the English method does not do. I cannot therefore see the point of changing, as England did, a well-proven widely accepted technique for one which has no outstanding advantages. It is a question of paying your money and taking your pick except, of course, if you are Welsh!

The ruck very definitely starts five yards from the ball. Players must get into a low driving position so that they can hit the ruck with their shoulders. They should grab hold of a team-mate as they go in, hard, low and parallel to the touch lines (Fig. 16). In coaching practice I often use a long bamboo cane, hold it at an appropriate height and insist that players get their heads and shoulders below it when joining the ruck. It does produce the body position which is crucial to good rucking.

The first men up must aim to drive beyond the man and ball. They must try to get under the opposition and keep driving forward (Fig. 17).

Fig. 16. Good body position is crucial to rucking.

The whole technique can be summed up thus: hit the ruck from behind the ball, bind tight, keep low and drive—picking the knees up helps leg-drive. Drive over the ball without touching it: if this cannot be done because of opposition resistance, then the ball should be scraped back with the feet.

Fig. 17. Aim to drive beyond the ball without touching it.

If winning possession is to be regarded as the foundation stone of the game, then using it should be regarded as the superstructure. It is the superstructure which is seen and on which an assessment of the whole is made. Do not forget, however, that the superstructure even though efficient can be deadly dull. On the other hand it can be both functional and a thing of beauty—a means by which the architect has expressed himself. We should think of using possession in these latter terms. We need to do it positively and effectively but at the same time players with flair, like the architect, must be allowed the opportunity of freedom of expression.

You might think that there is a hint of criticism in what I have stated. There is intended to be. I mentioned earlier in this book when discussing the philosophy of the game that many coaches and teams are accepting winning as the only priority, and that their views on the game do not measure up to the way in which they play it on the field. In other words they play a limited unambitious kind of Rugby which, by our standards, is rather dull and uninteresting. If we do not do something about it then British Rugby, which has long been famous for its back play, will lose a feature of its game which has been widely admired. Our standards have improved in Britain because we have worked, and we needed to, at organising our ball-winning potential; but for too many people this has become the end rather than the beginning. The result is safety-first Rugby and a lack of flair, initiative and imagination. This is not a matter of technique and skill but rather of philosophy and attitude. I recollect, a little while ago, castigating a friend of mine for the quality of Rugby played by a particular international team who had marvellous ball-winning capacity but whose ball-using skill was non-existent. I wanted to know why they could not be more ambitious, and my friend replied, "It's not in the nature of the beast." He meant, of course, that they were a cautious group, both players and coach. It only supports a view I have that Rugby is a means by which individuals, groups, yes, even nations express their personalities.

Using possession must not be regarded solely as the domain of the backs: forwards too must realise that in open play they are just players and, as such, they may be required to run, handle and make decisions just as any back does. This being so, all players whether backs or forwards must understand the principles of attack and defence and in particular the implications of gain and tackle lines. They are probably best illustrated in diagrammatic form, and reference to Figs. 18, 19 and 20 tells the whole story.

In Fig. 18 we have a situation where it can be said that there is a stalemate, but let me clarify the position. The gain line is an imaginary line which passes through the ball source and parallel to the goal line, i.e. through scrum, line-out, ruck and maul. Fig. 18 shows clearly that at the scrum the halfway line is also the gain line. Crossing the gain line is a key factor for effective team play. However, there is the tackle line to contend with as well, and this very often produces problems. The tackle line is that line on which opposing players meet. In Fig. 18 because the backs are equidistant from the gain line, the gain and tackle lines coincide, but more explosive running on the part of the attacking team would allow them to cross the gain line before they meet the tackle line. This should always be a first priority.

Let us now look at Fig. 19. This is much nearer the reality of the likely situation in a game. Defending teams are not generally as free with space as the defending team in Fig. 18, consequently they tend to line as near to the gain line as they can, taking off-side laws into consideration. Here we see that the defending Black team will cross the gain line long before the White attackers can reach it. In these circumstances the tackle line is said to be superior. If White backs run and pass in this situation they will be

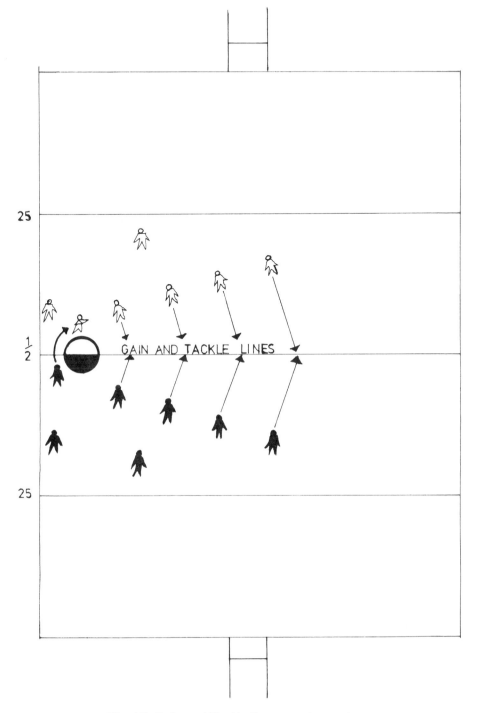

Fig. 18. Gain and Tackle lines causing stalemate.

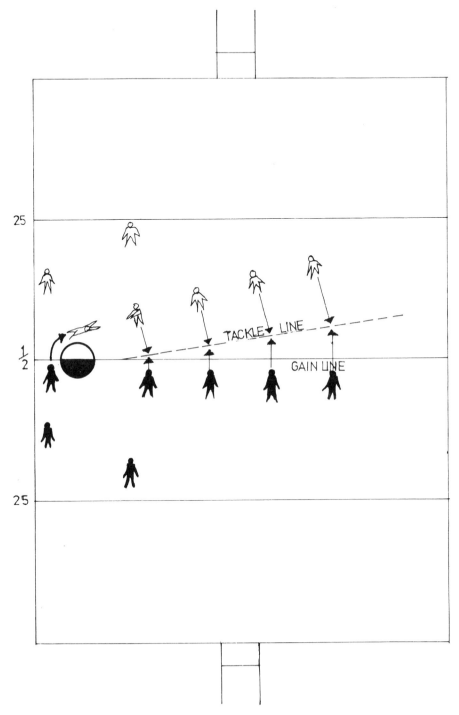

Fig. 19. Tackle line superior.

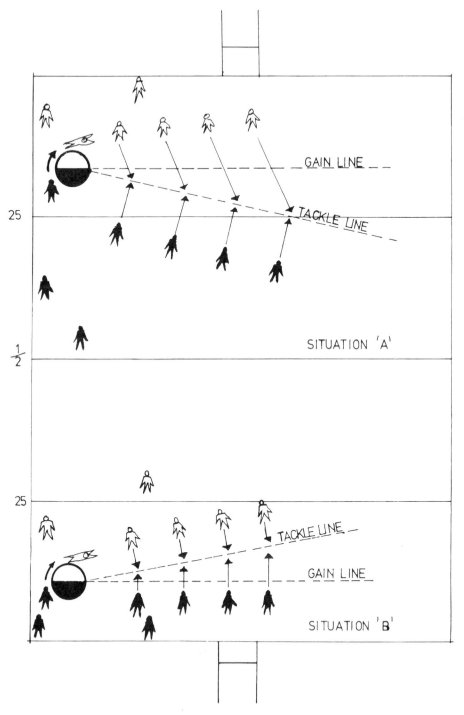

Fig. 20. Movement of the tackle line.

ineffective, unless in some way they can break the tackle line or force it backwards. Any tackle successfully made will allow Blacks to run forward to the tackled ball and the possible resultant ruck/maul. Whites, however, having won possession but used it ineffectively, will be forced to run backwards to the next phase of play.

It is probably Fig. 20 which is of great significance. In situation A it would appear that Whites are not well placed, because of their position in the field, to launch an attack. However, when it is analysed it will be seen that the opportunity for attack is favourable. Blacks, because they are in Whites' 22-metre area have lined fairly deep. If Whites can produce good ball they can obviously cross the gain line long before Blacks can reach it. Why then do not many more teams attack when they are in this position? There are probably two reasons. The first is that they do not understand the gain and tackle line concept, and therefore they tend to play the game according to their geographical position in the field. Second, they probably do not have enough confidence in their ability to run and handle and so clear the ball away. Safety first becomes the keynote and it is rather an uninspiring banner.

The reverse is true of Situation B. Whites would appear to be well placed for a running and handling back movement. However, on closer examination it can be seen that they will have to break the tackle line before they can cross the gain line. In these circumstances they would be well advised to try something other than an orthodox back line attack.

These then are the principles of attack and defence. They should be understood by all players. This is not to say that players must follow them slavishly, but they do, in general terms, indicate what may or may not be possible. There is little point in attempting something where the odds are weighted heavily against success. On the other hand there are players whose reaction and perception is so acute that they can confound all the theorists. These are the players with flair and initiative, they are especially valuable in using possession. The good coach will encourage them and allow them the opportunity to express themselves within the team framework.

It has always been said that the finest sight in Rugby football is to see the wing score a try in the corner—it had to be the corner because the opposition were in hot pursuit! The first thing we must understand is that this is a British concept. I doubt that a New Zealander would have the same image. In the Land of the Long White Cloud most young players dream of being a Colin Meads, a Kel Tremain or a Brian Lochore. British Rugby dreams are filled with Gareth Edwards, Barry John, Gerald Davies, David Duckham, Michael Gibson, J. P. R. Williams and J. J. Williams. It is a fact that we think differently about the game and this is reflected in the way we play it.

I also believe that international Rugby in the past ten years has produced some of the finest Rugby that has ever been seen. I do not have any experience of Rugby before the War but I have been a Rugby player and student since shortly after it. I recollect that in the fifties and sixties the quality of Rugby was poor, we seemed to have lost our way. Ken Jones, a great Welsh wing, played 44 times for Wales and scored 17 tries. He went match after match and hardly touched the ball. More recently Gerald Davies, with 24 caps as a wing (and another 13 as a centre), has scored 18 tries from this position. John J. Williams, with 15 caps, has already scored 9 tries. Without doubt the game has changed—for the better.

Few people would argue that the game has not improved, but still there is a feeling that back play is not what it was. This is a correct assessment, but that does not mean that it is worse, it merely means that it is different. Wings, at least Welsh wings, are scoring many more tries than they have ever scored. They are achieving what we have always regarded as the ultimate, and yet there is among many people this feeling that the game has lost something somewhere. In particular they are looking for the centres with the incisive sidestep and the slashing outside break—the Bleddyn Williams, the Jeff Butterfield and others of similar ilk.

The facts are that back play has changed; it has, like the rest of the game, become more organised and as such may demand a different kind of expertise. Good centres now are often referred to as the "organisation" men. An outstanding example—the outstanding example—of such a player in recent years is John Dawes. A superb passer of the ball, excellent tackler and a player who was the "oil-can" of the team; ally these to his qualities as a captain and you have a player of rare quality. Even John Dawes, however, was not fully appreciated, he was a player's player. The Rugby spectators tend to look for somebody who causes them to gasp, either at his sizzling acceleration or inside break. This is not to say that this kind of player cannot be an "organisation" man too. I have already mentioned Bleddyn Williams—he was one of the most complete of players, but of course in his day the pattern of the game was different. Nowadays, "overlap" is the "in" thing and it is achieved by miss passes or by the running full back, both virtually unheard of 20 years ago.

This is not to say that back play cannot be improved. There is a lot of evidence to suggest that coaches do not give enough attention to the coaching of backs. Perhaps this is why so often a team's ball-using ability does not match its ball-winning ability. If coaching is concerned with the pursuit of excellence then it must be all-round excellence, not just that of part of the team. The WRU Coaching Advisory Committee is currently engaged in writing a paper on back play because it is felt that coaches need guidance on the matter. Some people feel too that the over-lap technique is being too easily read, and that mid-field players in particular should rethink their options. Rarely now do we see the mid field (i.e. outside half and centres) taking on their opposite numbers unless it is the crash ball. Running skills need to be encouraged, not in any attempt to recapture something that was, but rather to add to the armoury of players so that when problems are posed they will have more than one answer.

The first question we have to ask is, "What do we require from the back line unit?" Ultimately, of course, we require the backs to score tries, but then my philosophy argues that this is what we ultimately want from forwards too. I am referring to a back line's *first* objective. Years ago I remember asking a Welsh international back line what was their first objective as a unit, and I got five different answers from seven people! It rather exploded the idea that Rugby is a team game. I believe that the first aim of the back line is to cross the gain line or, expressed in another way, to get in front of the forwards.

Backs must understand that the principles of play apply to them as much as they do to forwards, and therefore they must aim to go forward, to support, to maintain continuity, and when the opposition have the ball to put them under pressure. This is especially true in what would appear to be unfavourable areas of the field viz. gain and tackle lines, but most of all backs should be aware of the possibilities of counterattack.

Counterattack is an aspect of the game which has become increasingly important because it means that a team has virtually been given the ball by the opposition. It can come from a dropped pass, but more usually the opportunity to counterattack comes from a badly directed kick and it is most frequently, but not always, backs who have to deal with the situation. Successful counterattack is as much a matter of attitude as it is of skill, and it is backs in particular who must be aware of the possibilities. They have the opportunities to turn defence into attack and they must quickly assess the ball-using options. Sometimes, of course, counterattack is not possible for a number of reasons, but this is where the judgement (a part of skill) of the player who makes the decision comes in.

The essence of back play is running, passing, kicking and tackling, and as these are basic individual skills it is impossible to have a good back-line player who cannot perform, as a minimum, at least one of these skills superbly well. The outstanding player, naturally, is usually excellent at all of them. Good back play is therefore much more dependent on a higher individual skill level than good forward play. For instance in scrum, line-out, ruck or maul a particular individual weakness is much more easily accommodated by the unit and without necessarily detracting too much from the unit performance. In the backs, however, the weak individual is exposed and his performance, if it is inadequate, immediately affects the performance of the back-line unit.

This immediately poses problems for the coach because a back line can only be as good as its weakest member. Coaches, too, have tended to put more emphasis in coaching forwards, and backs are often left to fend for themselves. There is a real need for a better balance of coaching as between forwards and backs. In spite of individual limitations every player, with organised and purposeful practice, can improve, and in doing so make a better contribution to the team effort.

The problem lies in organisation. It is more difficult to organise back play in a practice session. There are many more facets to forward play and it is easier to "ring the changes". Back play too, demands very high quality work and makes much greater demands on anaerobic fitness, which in turn creates problems in terms of continuous repetition. One thing is certain: backs will only learn to cope with the actuality of the game if they are subjected to pressure in the practice session. Working slowly in a pressure-free situation is no way to prepare for a Rugby football match. Therefore, the imagination of the coach will be taxed in order to make the back's practice session both interesting and functional.

The key factors of back play can be summed up under:

1. Possession
2. Position
3. Pace.

POSSESSION

This relates to the ability of the individual and the unit to retain the ball. The poor pass or the poor kick is the certain way to lose possession. The incorrect decision as to whether to run, pass or kick can again put possession in jeopardy. Perhaps the most important point to emphasise in this connection is that of concentration. It is surprising how often possession is lost because of lack of concentration and a coach must continually urge his players to concentrate, otherwise he will never get the high degree of accuracy necessary for effective back play. Most people are amazed to learn that the 1971 Welsh backs, among the most talented of all time, comprising J. P. R. Williams at full back, Gerald Davies and John Bevan on the wings, John Dawes and Arthur Lewis at centre and Gareth Edwards and Barry John at half back, spent their time in practice concentrating on passing with pin-point accuracy to a target area. It certainly paid dividends and kills the idea that quality is achieved through a series of complicated movements.

POSITION

Position is a vital factor in effective back play. It not only refers to alignment in attack and defence but also to the disposition of the back line relative to the scrum, line-out ruck and maul and the options which may accrue. Let me first deal with alignment. The overall principle is that of a straight line both in attack and defence. In attack a straight line makes for a much smoother working of the back-line unit, while in defence a breaking of the straight line allows the opposition openings which if exploited can create real problems (Fig. 21).

In this context, too, perhaps I should refer to the angle of the back line when related to the gain line. I have never been an advocate of the "steep" angle. Some authorities have suggested that there should be a straight line between outside half, centres, wing and corner flag. This should result in a flat line near to one's

Fig. 21. The Barbarians *v.* Australia 1975. The Barbarians move up in defence—an almost perfect straight line.

goal line, and a very steep one near to the opposition goal line. This idea, however, totally ignores which team is in possession of the ball, and the whole concept of gain and tackle lines. If the first priority is to cross the gain line, lying steep from it does not help. In fact it pushes the tackle line even further back and makes for greater difficulty. I would advocate in attack a steepish angle from scrum half to outside half, but a much flatter angle from outside half to the open-side wing. It is also a convention for the open-side wing to lie level with the centres in attack so that he does not do too much unnecessary running, and to lie back in defence to cover the kick aimed behind the backs.

PACE

I have often referred to Fred Allen, the former All Black coach, stating that there was an answer to everything in Rugby except speed. Jeff Butterfield, an old friend and team-mate of mine, says that one of the objectives of a back is to try to interest two members of the opposition. Therefore they agree completely that

speed or pace is an essential attribute for good back play. However, it is not just running pace; of equal importance is ball pace,
because speed of accurate passing will always beat the runner no
matter how fast he is. Then too we have speed of thinking, reading
the situation and reacting accordingly. These are the three areas
where pace is of utmost importance to backs.

Within the back-line there are sub-units whose role is important and whose functions often overlap. The sub-units are half-
backs, midfield and the back three. I now intend to discuss them in
some detail so that we can understand clearly how they are
expected to contribute initially to the back-line unit and ultimately
to team performance.

THE HALF BACKS

The scrum half and outside half are the key players in any team
because they are the links between forwards and backs, and because one or the other dictates the pattern of play. Decision making is therefore extremely important and the ability to read a game
is vital. They must recognise quality possession and be prepared
to use it effectively. However, it is too easy to become obsessed
with good ball. If a team has an indifferent pack then the half backs
have to learn to use ball which in the purist sense is less than good.

The scrum half is the pivot of the team, he is also the first
decision maker and it is crucial that his skill level should be high.
The higher his level of skills then the more options he has. He
must ideally be able to pass well, to run elusively and to kick
superbly. Furthermore, he has to be able to reproduce these skills
in a variety of pressure situations. He must appreciate the difference between scrum, line-out and ruck/maul ball because his
option selection can have an immediate effect on how his back-
line colleagues are able to play.

If the scrum half is the pivot of the team then the outside half is
the pivot of the back line. Again he must be able to pass, run and
kick superbly well. He is most usually the man who "calls the

moves" and again his assessment of the situation—his judgement—is very important. Some people criticise the fact that a
"move" is called on every ball. How else can you play? There has
to be a general plan and this involves making a call on every set-
piece ball, even if it is merely a quick transfer to the wing. The
backs must know at every situation what is to be attempted,
otherwise they will have no chance whatsoever of playing together
as a unit.

The outside half must also appreciate the importance of set-
piece ball. I have already explained how, in my view, Rugby
thinking was greatly influenced in Great Britain by the 1967 All
Blacks, and in particular by their rucking expertise. To some
coaches, rucks and mauls became the most important part of the
game, and, on occasions, the only part. What they failed to realise
was that the All Blacks won such good set-piece ball that rucks
were created in most advantageous positions. My belief is that set-
piece ball is still the more important because it is from such
situations that all other phases of play originate. It is therefore
essential that an outside half should be able to play the set pieces
well.

The outside half must in the same way as the scrum half
appreciate the difference between scrum, line-out and ruck/maul
ball. This will obviously affect the moves that are called. In
general terms scrum ball is best exploited by the switch, the inside
cut, the crash ball. This is because of the proximity of the opposing backs. Line-out ball on the other hand lends itself to the
overlap, to the outside break, to the miss pass, to the full back
coming in and attempting to put an outside man clear. I have often
been critical of backs, even Welsh international backs, who select
a switch pass as an option off line-out ball. In my opinion it does
not work and I have the statistics to prove it. I have seen this
move attempted by Wales in many international matches but only
once have we scored a try and on nearly every other occasion we
have lost possession. This move is inappropriate because the
switch nearly always puts the ball back into opposition forwards.

The ball-carrier gets sucked in and that is usually the end of that! I feel that the percentage of success through switching line-out ball is so low that as a move it should be considered very carefully.

There is no doubt in my mind that ruck/maul ball should be moved quickly into open space. In other words, the scrum half must not run with it. Defences at ruck/maul are usually disorganised, and to take advantage of this the ball must be moved away. Of course there are always exceptions, a player like Gareth Edwards is so quick and strong that ruck/maul ball to him especially close to the opposition goal line is like manna from heaven. He has scored many tries in this way. It only goes to show that no plan must be followed slavishly; that it is players on the field who take decisions, all the coach can do is to give them a variety of options.

THE MID FIELD
By the mid field I am referring to the outside half and the two centres. They must work as a unit. In many ways the greatest change in back play has taken place in mid field and especially at centre. All mid-field players in recent years have found it more difficult to make breaks, especially from set pieces. Some critics have therefore concluded that present-day centres are not as good as those of yesteryear. This is an unfortunate conclusion because the game is different and I have already suggested that perhaps a different kind of expertise is required. We must acknowledge that if we have spent more time organising the way in which we play, it applies to defence just as much as it does to attack. In this way it would be more difficult to make running breaks in the mid field. It is also very significant in recent years how good runners have moved from the centre to the wing in the hope of finding more space which will allow them to display their running skills. One can think immediately of Maurice Richards (Cardiff and Wales), Gerald Davies (Cardiff and Wales), David Duckham (Coventry

and England). And few people in Britain will be aware of the fact that Grant Batty (New Zealand) was also a centre before he moved to the wing.

Having said all this, it may be that there is a tacit acceptance among the mid-field players that the defence will be too good. Therefore there may be a tendency to ignore the running skills of side-step, swerve, change of pace etc., at the set pieces and so work only on the other options. If this is so it is unfortunate, for the ability to beat a man is still a basic requirement for any back. The coach should encourage mid-field players to "take on" the opposition at set pieces. I say set pieces because usually in open play there is no particular problem.

The priorities of being able to pass, run, kick and tackle still apply to mid-field players, although as far as centres are concerned being able to kick well is probably of lower priority. They must, however, be skilful (in the widest sense) passers of the ball. They must be good readers of the game and be able to assess "man-over" situations in an instant. If there is a criticism that can be made of modern centres it is that some of them overcommit themselves physically. They must appreciate the need to vary their options, for this keeps the opposition guessing and this is one of the aims of the game.

THE BACK THREE

The Back Three is a term which will be used in the WRU Coaching Advisory Committee's paper on Back Play. It postulates that in the modern game there is a need to regard the full back and both wings as a unit both in attack and defence, hence the term "The Back Three".

Possibly the most dramatic change in Rugby Football in the last ten years has been the role of the full back. The restrictions on kicking direct to touch has had a tremendous influence on full-back play. He has been forced to rethink his game and it could be that this player alone has been responsible for much of the exciting Rugby which we have seen. Prior to the Law changes, a full back was selected almost entirely on his catching and kicking skills, coupled with positional play. Tackling, for example, was very low down on the list. I know of several international full backs whose tackling potential was very limited and yet in the game at that time they were outstanding players.

As far as the modern full back is concerned the priorities now are catching, running and tackling. J. P. R. Williams is the supreme example of the catcher/runner/tackler full back. He is arguably the greatest player in that position that we have ever seen, but to add strength to my point his kicking does not consistently match up to the superb qualities of the rest of his game.

The wing is something of an enigma. Very often he is the quickest and most talented runner in the team, but he is all too rarely used. In some way we must rethink the wing's role, just as the full back's role was rethought. It is now the norm for a forward to throw in from touch. My argument was always that this change released the wing, and so created problems for the opposition. I recollect talking to Garrick Fay, the Australian lock, during the Australian tour of Great Britain in 1975–76. I had been to Australia in 1974 for a month to help them set up a coaching scheme. Garrick said to me that they got the idea of using the hooker to throw in the ball from me on my 1974 visit. He said that they had attempted to use the wing who was thus released. He and other Australians had been disappointed when they came to Britain that although the hookers threw in the line-out ball, the blind-side wings did virtually nothing other than hang about on the fringes. I felt that this was a salutary comment of how one's thinking can go astray. One of the main reasons for getting a forward to throw in the ball has been lost. We must make an effort to use the wings much more than we do.

Perhaps we will have more success if we regard the full back and wings as the back three, as players in a unit, each interdependent on the other. This is certainly true in counterattack situations and also in defence. An additional idea which will be put forward in the Back Play paper is that the mid-field players are basically creators while the back three could be regarded as strikers. If they can operate as a unit they will certainly be a powerful force and perhaps add a new dimension to back play.

Many people argue that the best way to defend is to deny posses-sion to the opposition, but this is a simplistic view. We just have to accept that the opposition will have the ball and we must work from this premise. Certainly by adopting a positive attitude it is possible to restrict the quality of possession and so limit the attacking potential. There must also be a clear understanding of gain and tackle lines, because they are important factors in the defensive situation.

Prior to the Wales/France game in Paris in 1971 both Cliff Jones, Chairman of Selectors and Clive Rowlands, Coach to the Welsh XV, stressed the importance of tackling. The theme of the team talk became "tackle, tackle, tackle". It is a good beginning to a discussion on defence. Any team going out on the field imbued with that kind of spirit is going to be difficult to beat. I also believe that tackling is more a matter of heart than of skill.

However, I still think that defence is best summed up, as in principles of play, by the term "pressure". A team cannot tackle the opposition at a scrum, ruck or maul, but they can put them under pressure; perhaps by an eight-man shove or a wheel; per-haps by a drive at ruck or maul. In other words they can deny the opposition space, they can deny them time, they can subject them to pressure and this is what often causes them to make mistakes. This must be the object of any team when their opponents have the ball.

It is a basic direct approach to defence, but there are some people who tend to complicate the matter by devising complicated defensive patterns. Just after the War B. H. Travers, an Australian at Oxford University, wrote an excellent book entitled *Let's Talk Rugger*. Travers, now a distinguished Sydney headmaster, developed a system of defensive play which was to dominate British Rugby thinking for many years. He was the great exponent of "corner-flagging". He argued that the back line was the first line of defence, but by getting forwards to cover behind and towards the corner flag it was possible to set up second and third defensive lines. He convinced a lot of people, me included.

I worked on the principle of corner-flagging in my early coaching career, and when my team lost possession at a set piece I instructed my forwards to "corner-flag". While it was true that they set up a defensive cover which was difficult to beat, we hardly won any loose ball. This was hardly surprising because all my forwards were running backwards and on many occasions away from the ball. I do not know whether I misinterpreted Travers' ideas but I certainly began to question them. The "crunch" came one day in a practice match between my school first and second XVs. One team got the ball away and the opposition forwards began to corner-flag. The ball, however, got no further than the inside centre, who was tackled. A loose scrum (in those days) formed but one of my corner-flagging locks was yards away. I asked him in very direct terms what he was doing there. He replied, in equally direct terms, that he was there because that was where I had told him to go.

From that day on I never used the term "corner-flagging". I even insisted, years later, when the RFU *Guide to Coaches* was being written, that no reference should be made to "corner-flagging". I told my forwards that they should go where they thought the ball would be. I found this to be much more effective, for it taught players to anticipate, in other words it taught them to read the game. They reacted to reality and not in accordance with a pattern which may or may not be relevant to the game situation. Later of course I began to use the term "pressure", and I think that this is the most meaningful of all.

There are, however, specific jobs for particular players, especially back-row forwards. These have already been discussed earlier in the *Back Row* paper. There are different views on back-line defence, one pattern is that each back takes his opposite number, and I always feel this to be the soundest method. I often am asked the question of what advice I would give when perhaps an inside centre has made a break. Should he be allowed to run and should the defending outside centre and wing "shadow" their opposite numbers? It depends—but then it always does! My advice would be that from a set piece a player who makes a break should be allowed to run. The defenders should then shadow their opposite numbers and try at the same time to isolate the ball-carrier. The only qualification I make is that near to the goal line when a try is "on" it is policy to tackle the man with the ball.

My reasoning is that whether it is inside or outside, a break has occurred. Usually the inside break is less dangerous because it is nearer to the cover defence. The outside break is further away and more difficult to stop, therefore, for me, it is man-for-man marking. Remember, however, that for all the theories, tackle, tackle, tackle has much to commend it.

13 METHOD

Coaching method is probably the weakest area in the average Rugby coach's make-up. This, of course, is because many of them come from non-teaching backgrounds. When all is said and done the coaching of rugby football, at whatever level, is really an exercise in teaching, and therefore the fundamental principles of teaching are an essential background for the successful coach. The professional teacher naturally starts off with a big advantage, but that is not to say that all teachers make good coaches: some in my estimation are not all that clever at teaching either!

I should like to try to give some help to coaches who do not have a teaching background. A topic such as this merits a book on its own, but I am able to pick out only what I consider to be the key factors. The problem basically is to organise the club/school practice session and indicate some methods which will maximise the Rugby return in relation to the time available.

First of all let us consider the practice session and let us assume that there are 90 minutes available. Here then is a basic plan:

Section 1
20 mins.

Individual skills: After a brief warm-up the whole emphasis would be on pressure situations in handling, running, tackling, kicking etc.

Section 2
20 mins.

Unit Skills: Forwards would work on scrum or line-out or ruck/maul. Backs would develop attacks related to the work of the forwards. Both units should be expected to perform under pressure.

Section 3
20 mins.

Team Skills: The bringing together of forwards and backs to work with particular emphasis on what has been practised in Section 2.

Section 4   Team Practice: A short conditioned game trying to
15 mins.   produce under match conditions all that has
                previously been practised.

Section 5   Fitness: A pure fitness session—refer to Section III
15 mins.   for specific material.

Naturally this is merely a guide, it must be used intelligently according to particular needs and circumstances. It should be planned in relation to the way in which the team played in the last match, and also taking into account the kind of opposition to be met in the next match ahead. The coach has to be aware of the fact that it is a *team* practice session. Very often the individual has to be neglected in order to get the best out of all the players. Any individual weaknesses may need special attention. This cannot be given within the context of team practice. Therefore it is a good idea to arrange for specific skill clinics for certain players. They should come half an hour earlier than the others.

All the foregoing presupposes one vital factor on the part of the coach and that is PREPARATION. It is often the most neglected aspect of a club practice session, and it is often the state of unreadiness which causes the session to misfire. Careful preparation and planning is a must, and this is not only confined to the work actually done on the field. Included must be items such as notifying players of practice arrangements, seeing that changing rooms are open and that showers are available, apart from the more obvious things like providing balls, scrummaging machine, tackle bags, a properly marked-out practice area etc. Careful attention to this kind of detail will engender the confidence of all those taking part and this is obviously a good beginning.

The overall theme of the practice session must be Activity, Enjoyment and Purpose.

Activity

"Learning through activity" is an old teaching pearl and it is an excellent text for the Rugby coach. One of a coach's aims will be to improve the specific Rugby fitness of his player. There is no easy way, it can come only through hard work—through activity. This is also an easy way to produce discipline in the session; if players are continually being taxed physically they will have no opportunity to become bored or to "sky-lark". There is also another reason for activity, it is contained in the maxim, "You forget *most* of what you hear; you remember *some* of what you see but what you do, you *know*."

Enjoyment

It must not be thought that practice sessions are dull, dour affairs, where everyone is deadly serious contemplating the next game. Enjoyment has to be high on the list of priorities, after all this is the main motivating reason why people play Rugby football. The practice session is an excellent opportunity for developing team spirit and this chance must certainly not be neglected. Activity and enjoyment are really synonymous. In my experience, whenever you ask players at the end of a strenuous session whether they enjoyed it, the answer is invariably in the affirmative.

Purpose

The session must be purposeful, which means that it must be related to Rugby football; without purpose there can be no progress. It is perfectly possible to have an enjoyable physical session where the Rugby football content is low. This is obviously not making the best use of the time of the team. The aim of the coach therefore, must be purposeful practice.

TECHNIQUE, SKILL AND KEY FACTORS

In the beginning of this part of the book I made a reference to technique, skill and key factors because I felt it was necessary to define these terms at that time as I would be referring to them frequently in the ensuing chapters. These are the coach's coaching pegs. All his work will be "hung" on them. As a reminder I would re-emphasise that technique is merely a movement pattern, like passing a ball from A to B, but skill is applying that technique in the game: it is making decisions; it is demonstrating not only how to do something but when. Skill is all-embracing for it is the game itself.

As far as key factors are concerned, these are guide lines for the coach, they focus his attention on points which need to be examined if things are going wrong. They are not necessarily comprehensive but they are concerned with basic fundamentals and it is usually in this area that mistakes occur.

GRIDS

The use of grids in coaching has been widely accepted by a number of team games, notably Association Football. Only relatively recently have they been used in any sophisticated sense in Rugby football. Many Rugby coaches have unwittingly utilised the first principle of a coaching grid, that of restricting the working area, but have rarely developed the system. I am a great advocate of the grid system. John Dawes uses grids most effectively in National Squad sessions and I believe that any coach who ignores the idea is reducing his coaching potential.

There is no doubt that the proper use of a coaching grid can have a beneficial effect on the acquisition of skill and can accelerate the learning process. It can only do this, however, if it is properly understood. Using a grid can never make a poor coach a good one, but it can create a more favourable environment for learning and for acquiring specific Rugby fitness.

Perhaps I should begin at the beginning. A coaching grid is quite simply an area of field which is divided into squares. Usually ten-yard squares are most common, but there is no magic formula about this figure. It does, however, produce a reasonable working area. Activity then takes place in small groups in each square or combinations of squares.

This system produces a number of advantages. One of its greatest virtues lies in organisation, for it means that you can cope with large numbers in relatively small areas. For instance in an area 90 yards by 50 yards (a very small Rugby pitch) using six players to one square, you could cater for 270 players. I doubt that many coaches have to deal with this number but it does show you what is theoretically possible. Many clubs have the problem of only one pitch, and grass as we know reacts badly to overuse. Some coaching activities cause much more damage to the field than an actual game, therefore the in-goal area is one which lends itself particularly to grid work. Some time ago I did a practical session at one club with 35 players, and at the end what impressed them most was not the content of the session, but the fact that not once did we move out of the in-goal area. Another factor in its favour is the work-rate which coaches can generate by players operating in a confined area. Coupled with this is the control which can be exercised over the group.

Once the principle of grids has been accepted, they can be used in an infinite variety of ways. For instance, the activity can be a common one with everyone doing the same thing, or a variety of activities can be introduced. Again the emphasis can be on skill learning or on the specific fitness required for the game.

Let me give some examples of what I mean. Take the case of three players working together in one grid, passing the ball one to the other. They would be mostly concerned with "how" to pass. However, if we were then to allow one player to oppose the other two, whose task was still to pass the ball without dropping it or allowing the opponent to intercept, they now would be more concerned with "when" to pass—this is skill, the application of technique within the game. It is by far the most important aspect of coaching. As soon as we introduce opposition, players have to make decisions as they do in the game itself.

If, on the other hand, we wanted to work on specific Rugby fitness we would use the grid in a different way. By way of illustration I show a coaching grid which we have successfully

A – 3 v 3 passing game – no contact. See which team can keep possession longest.

B – Punting Tennis 3 v 3. Use 5 squares in line. The centre square is no man's land. No player may step in it and a ball landing in it counts against the kicker. The object is to kick the ball over the centre square to land in one of the opponent's squares. If it hits the ground the kicking team scores a point. The ball may be caught and kicked back and so on. Each player has three serving kicks which must be taken from within the end square.

C – Screen Pass – 6 players. Use the two end squares. 2 players each holding a tackle bag ten yards apart. 2 players, one with a ball and one supporter. 2 players resting. The ball carrier runs and drives shoulder first into the tackle bag, he screens the ball which is gathered by the supporter who runs around the tackle bag and runs to the other tackle bag followed by the original ball carrier and so on.
Five screen passes each, then the resting players become the tackle bag holders and the original tackle bag holders the ball carriers etc.

D – Circle Pass – 6 players. Players in a circle, one with a ball passes to any player, other than the ones on either side, and runs after the ball. The player catching passes and again runs after the ball and so on. Count the passes.

E – 2 v 1–3 players. Use two squares i.e. 20 yds. × 10 yds. 2 players with a ball try to score a try, the defender tries to stop them. Three tries each as ball carrier, supporter and defender.

F – Torpedo Throw Tennis – 3 v 3. As Punting Tennis above only torpedo throw instead of punt.

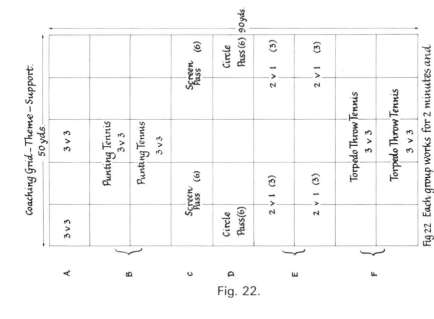

Coaching Grid – Theme – Support.

A	3 v 3		3 v 3	
B		Punting Tennis 3 v 3	Punting Tennis 3 v 3	
C	Screen Pass (6)			Screen Pass (6)
D	Circle Pass (6)			Circle Pass (6)
E	2 v 1 (3)		2 v 1 (3)	
F	2 v 1 (3)	Torpedo Throw Tennis 3 v 3	Torpedo Throw Tennis 3 v 3	2 v 1 (3)

50 yds.

90 yds.

Fig 22 Each group works for 2 minutes and then moves on to the next activity.

Fig. 22.

used on our Aberystwyth Courses. The theme is "support" and
the work rate is tremendously high. The plan of activities is set
out together with explanations of each activity (Fig. 22). In
Aberystwyth we work with large numbers, and this arrangement
will cater for 84 players working at one time, but I am quite sure
that it will easily be appreciated how the grids can be adapted to
suit much smaller numbers.

UNOPPOSED RUGBY

I have always been a bitter opponent of unopposed Rugby—in the
context of this chapter I suppose it ranks as "non-method".
Unopposed Rugby has a limited—very limited—contribution to
make to Rugby coaching. It occasionally may be useful to use no
opposition, merely to establish a pattern which everyone under-
stands. The trouble is that many coaches repeat a particular
movement without opposition *ad nauseam* in the mistaken belief
that they are teaching players how to play the game. This is a total
misconception. I liken unopposed Rugby to trying to play chess
against an opponent who has no chessmen. The chess player
reacts to his opponent, so does the Rugby player. In order to be in
a skill-learning situation there has to be opposition. It need not be
15 against 15, that often is as bad as 15 against 0, but it can be 15
against 3, against 6, against 9 etc. The sooner this idea is accepted
totally then the better coaching efforts will be rewarded.

Finally on method, let us not lose sight of the fact that coaches
are all different and whatever methods are used they are only a
means to an end. That end should be positive effective football.

SECTION III
Citius, Altius, Fortius

It is always sound policy to define one's terms so that when they are used everyone will know what is meant. I have always differentiated between "practice" and "training". The former, for me, is concerned with total preparation for the game, fitness, skill improvement, tactics etc. "Training", on the other hand, is confined entirely to physical conditioning. By my definition, therefore, the "club training evening" is a misnomer. I call it the "club practice evening" and training would be a part of it.

Rugby football is a game which makes very heavy demands on fitness resources, and fitness for the game is a prime factor if it is to be played well. Many players are prepared to work hard at acquiring skill, but they often hope to acquire enough fitness for the game merely by attending the club practice session. In other words they expect the club coach to get them fit. This is a concept I am not prepared to accept. Fitness is the individual's responsibility. The coach cannot afford to waste the time of the team on pure physical conditioning. It is doubtful whether any club meets more than twice a week for practice; if a large part of this time is spent on training, how do we improve our game? You could end up with a group of very fit players whose skill level and tactical appreciation were poor. In any event a well-structured practice session in itself makes heavy fitness demands and it is the duty of every player to present himself at the practice session with a high level of basic fitness. I am continually saying to coaches that their job is to take the basic fitness of individuals, and build on it the specific fitness required for the game. To players, my message is, "the fitter you are, the harder and longer you can practise; the harder and longer you practise, the better you become at the game".

Finally let me qualify the remarks I have made. As seen in

Section II of this book, pure fitness would feature in my club practice session but it would occupy no more than 10 to 15 minutes at the end of the session. Whatever the fitness responsibility vis-à-vis individual and coach and team and coach, one thing is certain; the coach must be well-informed and able to advise his players on training procedures.

Having apportioned responsibility for fitness there are some other questions which need posing. Why do we need to be fit for the game? What targets should we set in terms of fitness training? What kind and methods of training should we adopt to satisfy the game's demands? I hope to answer these, and in doing so present some guidelines from which individual players and coaches can benefit. However, they are guidelines and should be used as such. Let me make one thing clear at the outset. There is no easy way to achieve a high standard of fitness, in spite of what advertisements in many magazines would have you believe. Two sayings stand out in my mind. As a young physical education student I remember reading one of Pindar's ancient Olympic Odes. In it he said, "Without toil there have triumphed a very few." The second quotation, author unknown, is a modern version of Pindar's: "The only place where success comes before work is in the dictionary." When embarking on a fitness programme it is not a bad text to have before you.

The vast majority of players play Rugby because they enjoy it. I can think of no better reason. However, the physical demands of the game sometimes become so great that a player's fitness resources are taxed beyond the limit. This results in extreme discomfort and it is doubtful whether this state offers any enjoyment at all. Extreme fatigue sets in, which results in a lack of concentration and a consequent lowering of skill. Fatigue, too, exposes a player to a greater risk of injury. Higher basic fitness levels would make for greater enjoyment of the game, because a player would be operating within his physical capacity and not stretching himself beyond the limits of his capabilities.

The value of fitness therefore can be defined by the following objectives:

1. building up a resistance to fatigue;
2. aiding recovery after exertion;
3. increasing the capacity to learn skills;
4. preventing injury.

Building up a resistance to fatigue results in an increased capacity for work. It is obvious that this factor alone can have a beneficial effect on the game of any team. In terms of principles of play it means a higher degree of support and continuity. Expressed in another way we could say that the greater the work capacity then the higher the potential for skill. Note that I am careful to use the word potential because one cannot automatically equate work capacity with skill. However, one can say without any qualms that fatigue, when it sets in, causes a break-down in skill.

The nature of Rugby is such that the game is played in periods of intense activity interspersed with rest periods of varying intervals. The activity and rest periods are influenced by many factors; level of skill, fitness and attitude of both teams, weather and ground conditions, not forgetting the referee's interpretation of Law. Increased fitness can improve an individual's ability to recover from one period of physical exertion before he embarks on another. This means that his concentration is unimpaired and that his skill level will be higher. From a practical point of view I never let players I am coaching bend over and put their hands on their knees after a period of intense effort. If your opponents see you do that they they know that you are in trouble. As I say to my players, "Stand up and leave them guessing!"

The acquisition of skill is largely determined by an inherited capacity for learning, but many skills require a particular aspect of fitness before they can be performed well. Strength, for example, is a prerequisite for acceleration, side-step, making and resisting tackles, keeping the ball available, ripping in a maul and so on. I could of course give many other illustrations, but perhaps these are sufficient to make a case for developing high fitness levels in order to create the right environment for the development and production of skill.

The fourth objective of training is to give greater protection against injury. I have already stated that injuries often occur as a result of fatigue. They also occur, of course, as a direct result of contact—player with player and player with ground. Recent sports medicine surveys indicate that when compared with soccer, Rugby injuries tend to be more traumatic in terms of fractures and concussion but fewer in number where minor injuries are concerned. Further, Rugby produced more upper body injuries than soccer. One, however, would expect this because of the tackling and ground contact situations. Much can be done to strengthen the muscles surrounding joints and so perhaps make for greater protection. The shoulder joint in particular, in comparison with other joints, because of its great range of movement is relatively weak. Similarly the quadricep muscle (i.e. the large muscle on the front of the thigh) can, if strengthened, give considerable stability to the knee joint. Graham Adamson ("Training Methods"—*Physiotherapy* June 1972), a well-respected figure in the fitness field, suggests that no player should indulge in a contact sport unless he can perform a knee extension with a 50-pound weighted boot, ten times in 40 seconds.

What do we mean by fitness? On its own it has very little meaning, for it infers different things to different people. The World Health Organisation's definition of fitness suggests that it is "the ability to perform work satisfactorily under specified conditions". On the other hand Morehouse and Miller, two renowned American exercise physiologists, have defined it thus, "The term fitness implies a relationship between the task to be performed and the individual's capability to perform it." One can assume therefore, from these two statements, that fitness is specific, or more correctly task-specific. In essence it means that being fit for one sport does not necessarily imply fitness for another. Being fit for swimming does not make one fit for Rugby. In fact one could go further and say that in Rugby itself being fit to play at centre does not make one fit to play at prop. From the Rugby point of view fitness is being able to repeat the maximum tasks demanded without any undue feeling of stress. Before, however, we can train the various systems that contribute to performance, we have to be aware of the game's demands and how they are likely to affect players.

In general terms fitness for a specific sport demands:

(a) a high level of basic fitness. This type of fitness is dependent on the cardio-respiratory system and expresses itself in the ability to sustain intense activity for a long period of time, to delay the onset of fatigue and to recover rapidly;

and (b) a specific fitness peculiar to the sport, in our case, Rugby, which makes differing demands upon speed, strength, power, muscular endurance and agility.

In Rugby there are differing classifications within the game, i.e. tight forwards—strength; link men—strength, muscular endurance and speed endurance; three-quarters—speed and speed endurance.

More specifically the fitness requirements for the various positions could be classified as:

    1. Tight Forwards—scrummage, ruck/maul contact, support and protection against injury.
    (a) high degree of muscular strength—legs, back and arms;
    (b) cardio-respiratory endurance;
    (c) muscular endurance.

    2. Back Row Forwards—support at speed, strength at breakdown, protection against injury.
    (a) cardio-respiratory endurance;
    (b) speed and speed endurance (large work capacity at speed);
    (c) upper arm and shoulder girdle strength.

    3. Backs—penetration, contact and protection against injury.
    (a) speed and acceleration;
    (b) specific endurance to enable fast recovery between bouts of explosive running (cardio-respiratory endurance built through interval training);
    (c) local muscular endurance—legs;
    (d) shoulder girdle strength.

Fitness therefore, is dependent upon the foregoing factors, but we must not forget that fitness is specific and we must recognise this by training the various systems to adapt specifically to the imposed demands of the game. There is a basic training concept expressed as the SAID principle (Specific Adaptation to Imposed Demands). It embraces the training principles of overload, specificity and reversibility which I will discuss later.

DEMANDS OF THE GAME

We have heard on many occasions of the players of yesteryear; how fast they could run, how far they could kick, how high they could jump in the line-out, how strong they were. This, however, is all subjective opinion. There is very little fact to substantiate what is said. I am sure that they were, of their time, great players but comparison with the present day player is impossible. One thing is certain, and that is, that in general, the modern player is much fitter, and I draw this conclusion from the vast improvement in performance in other sports which are entirely objective such as athletics, swimming, weight lifting etc. I cannot believe that games players have been left behind in the ever-rising fitness levels. However in the final analysis I cannot prove it because there is no data.

Therefore, when we examine the demands of the game, we have to do it in an objective pattern so that we can obtain information and relate a training pattern to it. This is not easy and requires a very detailed study. Henry Coupon of France in correspondence with E. Gwyn Evans of Wales has revealed some interesting information as a result of some recent investigations. It gives us an insight into the mechanical structure of the game. It reinforces some of the very modest work which Gwyn Evans and I have done from time to time and upon which we have based a lot of our fitness work. Henry Coupon's findings are much more detailed and do provide a basis from which valid training procedures can be programmed.

A game, although lasting 80+ minutes by the referee's watch, has only 27 minutes of actual playing time, made up on average of 140 sequences of action. Coupon found that:

> 0–5 seconds made up 32% of the sequences
> 5–10 seconds made up 24% of the sequences
> 10–20 seconds made up 29% of the sequences
> 20–30 seconds made up 10% of the sequences
> 30–40 seconds made up 3% of the sequences
> 40–50 seconds made up 1% of the sequences
> 50 seconds and over made up 1% of the sequences.

From these figures we can see that:

> 56% of the activity patterns lasted less than 10 seconds;
> 85% of the activity patterns lasted less than 20 seconds.

The conclusion we can draw from this is that at least 120 sequences of play lasted 15 seconds. If we accept that fitness is specific then such a pattern must be reflected in our training. How often is this the case? There are on average 40 scrums in a game, 5 per cent last at least 10 seconds, and 90 per cent last 20 seconds; again we must train to accommodate such demands. A similar analysis in rucks and mauls showed that just over 70 per cent last up to 5 seconds, 24 per cent between 5 and 10 seconds, with the remainder lasting over 10 seconds. Figures reveal, too, that the ruck/maul situation forms almost 50 per cent of all phases of the game where players are contesting the ball. Teaching technique and developing skill, of course, become an integral part of this specific training pattern. Technique, skill and fitness are all important components which must be given consideration.

Coupon also found that scrum and secondary struggles for possession occupy almost 12 minutes of strong physical effort, mainly by forwards. The strength demand is obvious, it must be given attention. The backs are involved in this kind of situation much less frequently so the balance of training should take this into account.

We must remember that Rugby is not merely concerned with work only. The pattern really is one of work/rest/work. Training is geared to this pattern as well, but specificity dictates that the period of rest should be related to that experienced in the game. One of the purposes of training is to delay the onset of fatigue, and controlling work time and rest time (interval training) is one way of progressively adapting the physiological system to meeting and coping with demands in the game. The rest pattern in a game shows the following distribution:

0–10 seconds — 8·25%

10–20 seconds — 43·00%

20–40 seconds — 33·50%

40–60 seconds — 8·50%

60–80 seconds — 6·75%

80 seconds+ — 7·75%

Almost 84 per cent of rest intervals last not more than 40 seconds. It would appear therefore that a work/rest ratio of 20 seconds : 40 seconds is the norm to achieve.

Running patterns show a distinct difference between forwards and backs. Forwards appear to run about 6,000 yards at top club level, while the three-quarters average around 4,000 yards. As one would expect the link-men, i.e. back row and half backs, cover larger distances but with a greater proportion run at a fast pace. In fact international forwards cover one third of their total distance at top speed, and the rest at approximately three-quarter effort. Backs work more on a ratio of 50 : 50.

There is one other factor that we must bear in mind when organising practice/training programmes. Rugby football is a contact game. These external forces, player with player, player with ground, are very energy-sapping and this again must be reflected in the work done.

Coaches are concerned with training and coaching players to produce maximum performance in games. In order to achieve such an aim they must understand that high quality performance in Rugby results from the successful combination of skill, physical capacity and psychological adaptation under the conditions existing at the time. Astrand, a Swedish exercise physiologist, suggests that we look upon physical performance in terms of energy output, neuro-muscular function and the psychological attitude with which we approach competition.

Energy output is concerned primarily with the adequate supply of the type of energy needed for the duration of the game. We know that in Rugby the need is for short bursts of maximum output, relieved with spells of low output spread irregularly over a playing period of 80 minutes. Neuro-muscular function is the extent to which we can skilfully apply existing strength to the specific task demanded at the time. Motivation and tactics are the basic ingredients of psychological attitude. They are influenced by the level of competition, by prevailing natural elements and by known strengths and weaknesses of the teams in opposition.

PHYSIOLOGICAL CONSIDERATIONS

Energy Systems

I do not propose to go into long and involved details concerning the physiology of exercise. The research workers have over the years produced evidence which is of great interest to those working for an improvement in physical performance. It is the conclusions with which we should be familiar rather than the methods by which they were achieved. I will therefore try to give a very brief explanation concerning the provision of energy for particular types of physical effort required for good performance.

Metabolism is the process by which foods are broken down in the body and either converted into energy or stored in the body. The main source of energy for muscular contraction, which is essential before any kind of movement can take place, is carbohydrate and fat from consumed food. This straight away has implications for those players who think that eating steak (high in protein, low in carbohydrate) before playing in a match is a means of providing energy. Protein is normally a rebuilding food and is rarely used as a fuel for muscular contraction. Let us regard food as the basic fuel which runs the human machine. There is evidence to support the premise that free fatty acids provide the major fuel source in low intensity exercise, whereas the harder the effort the more dependent is the body upon glycogen as the main source of fuel.

This suggests that there are two main energy systems. Indeed there are, one is called the aerobic system while the other is the anaerobic system. Coaches need to have a simple understanding of their functions because training programmes should be related to them. Aerobic fitness is concerned with the provision of energy for long-term work and is associated with the ability of the circulatory system to transport oxygen from the lungs to the working muscles. It is an exercise state whereby the oxygen supplied is equal to the demand in the muscle, and other words it is a balanced position. The body's capacity for transporting and utilising oxygen is limited, but through training it is possible to improve such capacity by as much as 20 per cent.

One of the disadvantages of the aerobic system is that it is slow to adjust to energy demands and can, depending upon the intensity of exercise, take up to three or four minutes before it adjusts to the demand for oxygen. Fortunately the body can bring in its alternative quick-energy supply—the anaerobic system—which can produce immediately energy in the absence of oxygen.

However, nothing is perfect and the use of the anaerobic system has one big draw-back: the production of toxic waste in the form of lactic acid. The presence of lactic acid leads to muscle fatigue. When a muscle's optimum tolerance level to an accumulation of lactic acid is reached, then the level of activity must slow down so that the aerobic system takes over. If this is not done then everything grinds to a halt. Even after the cessation of activity an increased oxygen uptake is required by the body. This is because it needs to repay the "oxygen debt" which has been incurred. It is known that world-class athletes in certain events are able to build up huge oxygen debts, i.e. tolerate high levels of lactic acid.

What are the implications of all this for Rugby? Aerobic power can be increased through training, usually in the form of distance running, fartlek-type training and long interval runs. The trained aerobic system affords the opportunity to work at high levels without having to utilise anaerobic power. This means that much work can be done without developing toxic wastes. Increasing one's aerobic capacity therefore, has distinct advantages for the Rugby player.

The anaerobic system, too, can be trained in that the body can learn to tolerate lactic acid build-up. This is achieved by participating in activities which induce high levels of lactic acid, e.g. interval and paarlauf runs, circuit training etc.

Rugby players use both these systems to a great extent since, as we have already seen, the demands of the game are for short intensive periods of activity coupled with slow jogging in recovery or when repositioning is necessary. The evidence shown also suggests that Rugby is a game which primarily uses anaerobic power for providing energy, so that the training of this system through work/rest/work ratios is of paramount importance. It is probable too, that improvement in anaerobic fitness is to some extent dependent upon aerobic power, because in the long term it is the supply of oxygen available that is the key factor both during activity and recovery. It would be logical therefore to work towards influencing and training both energy systems.

Neuro-muscular Functions

Strength Rugby players are particularly dependent upon strength as a factor in their ability to play well. We can define it as the means of exerting force. In fact there are two kinds of strength:

(a) static;
(b) dynamic.

Static strength is the ability to apply force in a position where there is no movement. Forwards holding a "lock" position in the scrum provide a good example of the use of static strength. Dynamic strength, which is more often seen, is that type of strength where the force overcomes the resistance and we see movement.

Strength is directly linked with the cross-sectional area of muscle fibres. During contraction to overcome resistance, muscle fibres contact totally, but if the resistance is weak then not all the fibres are required to work. Where muscles are not subjected to hard work they lie in the dormant, untrained state. Working muscles against progressive resistance will lead to greater strength development and those fibres brought into play will increase in size. As the loads become progressively heavier more and more muscle fibres are engaged in action and ultimately the whole muscle increases in size.

As I have already stated strength is a highly important factor in the game. I remember some years ago talking to Barry John when he was a player and he was rather doubting the value of strength training. I asked him, "What is wrong with being strong?" He could not answer that one so he said, "OK, strength training it is." No player can be too strong for Rugby, but he has to learn to use his strength for a better performance in the game and this, of course, will be related to positional requirements. This kind of strength is best developed by heavy resistance work of a specified nature. Strength, too, contributes directly to other factors especially muscular endurance, power and agility.

Muscular Endurance This is the ability of the muscles to resist
fatigue during work which is usually localised. It depends to some
extent on the efficiency of the cardio-respiratory system in supply-
ing blood to the working muscles. However, absolute strength
would appear to be the main contributor to muscular endurance
or strength endurance. This can be easily illustrated by taking the
examples of two players, A and B. Let us say that their maximum
weight training load in a particular exercise is 100 pounds and 50
pounds respectively. If both were asked to perform the exercise as
many times as possible with a load of 50 pounds, player A would
obviously perform many more repetitions that player B for whom
it is a maximum. This is why absolute strength is such a crucial
factor in strength endurance.

Power Power is force times velocity, or in Rugby terms
strength applied at speed. To improve power you have to work on
these two factors. The speed of muscle contraction cannot be
greatly influenced by training, but fortunately enormous gains can
be made in strength, thus making for high power levels. Power is a
vital factor in Rugby and is associated with making and breaking
tackles, explosive acceleration, snap shove in a scrum and force-
fully ripping in a maul. When considering methods for improving power one needs to consider the strength/speed curve. If the
strength end of the continuum needs to be influenced then one
should be working in the area of 70 per cent of maximum
strength. If the speed end of the continuum needs influencing then
35 per cent maximum strength loads should be used. I shall say
more about these principles when discussing power training
methods. Of course one does not always need to use weights,
one's own body weight is a valuable aid and continuous hopping
and jumping for distance are very useful "power" activities.

Speed This is the quality every player wishes to have. I have
already quoted the saying of Fred Allen, the renowned coach of
the 1967 All Blacks, that, "There's an answer to everything in

Rugby football except speed." Basic speed is undoubtedly a very great asset but we need only concern ourselves with two factors which contribute to overall speed. They are

(a) acceleration speed

and (b) maximum running speed.

It is the former, the ability to accelerate rapidly over the first 20 metres, which is of greatest importance to most players. The latter is important to backs in general. It is possible of course to have one kind of speed and be lacking in the other. The fast runner whose acceleration is poor can improve his overall speed significantly because acceleration can be influenced through training. If the situation is reversed, however, the potential for improvement is not so good. The good accelerator who lacks real pace overall has relatively little room for improvement. Overall leg speed is extremely difficult to improve unless by highly specific training. It is also true to say that high-speed running requires a high degree of skill.

Speed Endurance   This is the capacity to resist fatigue from heavy anaerobic loadings in energy production. Such a situation often exists in Rugby where there is a period of continuous play involving long runs by players, especially backs. It is even more prevalent in seven-a-side. Training to improve this fitness quality requires near-maximum runs over 200–300 metres with relatively long rest intervals of three to four minutes.

Agility   The term requires little in the way of definition because most people know what it means. In Rugby we immediately think of the ability to change direction quickly by means of swerve, side-step and the ability to spring up quickly after a tackle. It is a complex element of fitness and is both general and specific. It can be improved, as can the majority of the fitness factors. Fatigue diminishes agility by having an adverse effect on its components like strength, speed, power and reaction time. It is therefore highly desirable that the oxygen transport system is trained to offset this deterioration. Excess body weight adds an unwanted burden and obviously affects agility. Players with excess weight should try a sensible programme of diet. The supreme example of the agility athlete in Rugby football is Gareth Edwards. He has without doubt the greatest range of personal skills that I have ever seen in a Rugby player, many of them based on his superb physical qualities.

Physical Limitations   Physical performance is limited by two factors—natural endowment and training. Heredity plays a major part in the selection of top-class players, in that many are born with a greater natural capacity than others. This is often seen early in a player's career. The possession of greater natural healthy weight, strength and speed are obvious physical attributes to playing the game successfully. This has to some extent been substantiated by an analysis of physical performance scores of young Welsh Rugby players which have been recorded over the years. Gareth Edwards, John Bevan (the 1971 Lion) and Roy Bergiers are outstanding examples of players who produced excellent standards in power measurement early in their playing careers.

However, it would be quite wrong to assume that height, weight and fitness are the sole limiting attributes in quality Rugby performance. Skill is undoubtedly the most important factor of all. When the WRU produced its paper on *Back Row Play*, critics said that all we were seeking were jumbo-size players. Such a statement bore no resemblance to the truth. The Welsh team for several years after the appearance of the paper had probably the lightest back row of the major Rugby Countries—Mervyn Davies (15 stone then), John Taylor (13 st 7 lb) and Dai Morris (an incredible 12 st 12 lb!).

Many factors contribute towards skilful Rugby, fitness is one of them, but all are interdependent to some degree and all probably limited to some extent by natural capacity. Nevertheless, accepting this limitation, training can improve performance in almost every respect thus modifying the natural differences, for training produces physical changes—particularly if based upon modern scientific principles. Modern training methods have helped players to realise aspirations which many consider to be beyond their reach. Such results however can only be achieved by determination and dedication to training. I am not saying, of course, that all players must train and dedicate themselves to the game. I recognise that Rugby for some is merely a means of relaxation: they have little ambition other than to enjoy themselves on Saturday afternoons and certainly such players will not be reading this book! There are, however, many more who are ambitious, who do want to improve and who are prepared to give up their time to do so. They deserve help and encouragement and must be given the kind of guidance which will ensure that they are not wasting their time.

It is for this latter reason that coaches and players need to be aware of certain training principles in order to obtain maximum value for effort and time. Once these are recognised, a course of training can be pursued which if it is progressive in intensity will lead to improvement. The rate of improvement will not only be governed by volume and intensity of training but also by skill and fitness levels apparent at the beginning of such training.

To sum up, the physical elements we hope to influence are:

1. cardio-respiratory endurance;
2. muscular strength and endurance;
3. speed of running—acceleration—agility;
4. power—the ability to use strength at speed, more recently referred to as "elastic strength".

17 TRAINING PRINCIPLES AND PROCEDURES

Faulkner expounds certain fundamental principles of training and they are based upon:

1. Overload
2. Specificity
3. Reversibility.

Overload

The theory of overload postulates that for muscle cells to increase in size or function they must be taxed to the limit of their present capacity. It also means that as the efficiency of the muscle increases then the training intensity too has to be increased. Systematic progression is the method by which intensity is increased. Initially loads of below maximum capacity should be used and then gradually added to in successive training sessions.

Specificity

This principle maintains that training is specific to the cells (physiologically everything takes place at this level) and to the specific structural and functional element within a cell that is overloaded. That is to say, you only improve when you follow the precise principle of training which applies to the desired outcome, e.g. training to improve the high energy system through short sprints of 30–40 yards with 25–30 seconds rest will not specifically improve ability to resist an accumulation of lactic acid. Longer runs are needed. Likewise, you cannot train for speed without actually running fast.

Reversibility

This principle contends that the effects are transient. One tends to lose qualities at the speed with which they were gained. Many players, having worked hard to produce certain qualities during the season, cease activity when the season ends and so lose the hard-won benefits. Some alternative activity would ensure a certain basic level of fitness which could then be a platform for the following season.

Warm-Up

A period of warm-up should precede any vigorous activity, since the body appears to function better and it affords some measure of protection against injury. Some physiologists suggest that without a warm-up, the muscles most frequently injured are the "antagonists" to the strong flexing muscles. A short period of general running, stretching and twisting movements should be undertaken before starting a game. Such a warm-up could be a part of the organised practice/training session.

Flexibility

There is some evidence to suggest that increased flexibility in the hip joints can lead to slight increases in stride length if utilised correctly. To this end the following exercise might prove to be of benefit:

Stand with one leg forward and the other back, as wide as possible, sink down into a lunge position by bending the front knee over the forward foot. Keep the rear leg straight. When in the full lunge position, squeeze the body weight down, make a conscious effort to relax the muscles being stretched. The squeeze should be gentle, but taking the muscles to a full stretch position which should be held for two seconds. Repeat five to ten times (increase repetitions gradually) and then repeat with legs in alternate positions. Keep the body upright. A slight backward lean should help to stretch the iliapsoas muscle. Excessive shortening of this muscle is often a source of lower back complaints.

Nutrition

Nutrition is a study in itself but the following nutritional principles as applied to training would seem to be valid.

1. A normal well balanced diet adjusted in terms of calory input when activity is increased is considered to be adequate to meet the needs of athletes. The addition of special nutrients for improving performance does not appear to have much scientific backing.

2. There is some evidence to support an additional intake of glucose syrup when participating in activities of an endurance nature. Some players in the 1976 Welsh team took Dynamo— a glucose syrup drink especially made for athletes etc.—both before the game and during half-time. They thought it beneficial.

3. During pre-season training when strength gains are being sought or during normal growth periods an increased intake of protein might be of some benefit.

4. I have already condemned the practice of eating steak before a match. It is largely protein which is not an energy provider, and in any event some authorities say that it can take between 10 and 18 hours to be digested properly. Carbohydrate in the form of toast and honey for example would be of much more value. Provided he eats early enough before a game and bearing these points in mind, a player should follow his own dictates.

5. Eating is a habit and a high food intake can cause problems when a player ceases to play. A great deal of discipline is required in order to balance food intake with energy output, otherwise there may be excessive gains in weight.

TRAINING PROCEDURES

Endurance (Aerobic-Fitness)

It has been established by Cooper* that in devising a training programme to influence the cardio-respiratory system two principles need to be observed:

1. If the exercise is vigorous enough to produce a sustained heart rate of 150 beats per minute or more, the training effect benefits begin about five minutes *after* the exercise starts and continues as long as the exercise is performed.

2. If the exercise is not vigorous enough to produce or sustain a heart rate of 150 beats per minute but is still demanding oxygen, the exercise must be continued considerably longer than five minutes, the total period of time depending on the oxygen consumed.

The implications of these statements are clear: in order to build up aerobic capacity, coaches and players should make use of pulse counts. These provide a clear indication that the work loads are being achieved. Probably the easiest place to find a pulse beat is by locating the carotid artery (just above the collar bone and alongside the wind pipe). The count should be taken *immediately* after the cessation of exercise. Count for ten seconds and multiply by six. This will give a reasonably accurate figure for heart rate during exercise.

Obviously, one's initial state of fitness determines how high the heart rate will rise during activity. A distance runner will need to run at a much faster pace than a fit or unfit Rugby player in order to keep his heart rate above 150 beats per minute. Of course there is a training effect at lower heart rates and indeed initially, during pre-season training sessions, it would be as well to work on slower

* Cooper, K. H., "A means of assessing maximal oxygen intake." *Journal of American Medical Assn.* 203.

Run / Walk Endurance Programme.

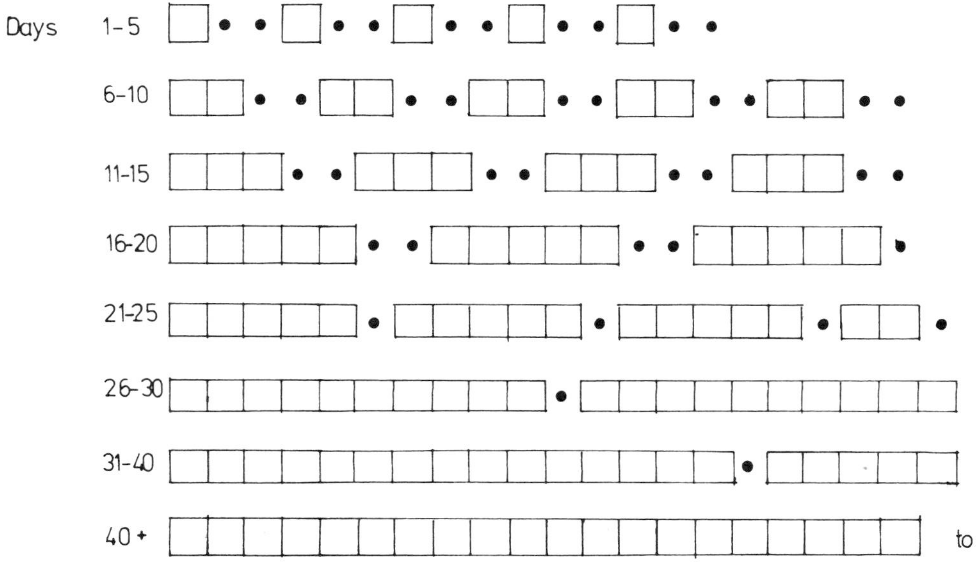

Fig. 23

Exercise 3 – 4 times per week

Days refer to actual exercise days ie. days 1–5 schedule should be adhered to for the first five exercise sessions.

to be run at varying speeds of fast and slow after the 6th minute.

Days

| 1-5 |
| 6-10 |
| 11-15 |
| 16-20 |
| 21-25 |
| 26-30 |
| 31-40 |
| 40+ |

☐ = 1 min jogging

● = 1 min walking

runs over longer periods. This also puts less strain on the muscles and tendons of the lower leg. This kind of fitness can be achieved through a combination of running and walking if fitness levels are low. The Run/Walk Endurance programme (Fig. 23) provides an easy progression even for the most unfit player. Improvement is usually quite quick providing regular exercise is taken and progression is controlled. Progression is important, overload principles should be observed in terms of increased running time, or increased pace or shorter rest intervals or a combination of all three.

The Run/Walk programme for players who keep active during the close season will probably be too easy. In such cases they can miss out the first 15 days and state at stage 16–20. In this way they will be attempting a 20-minute continuous run in about four weeks. Pulse rates must be checked to ensure that they are working hard enough to produce a training effect. If not, then a faster progression and/or more intensive work are indicated. I would recommend all players to keep active during the close season, otherwise reversibility takes over and much hard work is needed merely to regain that which was lost, let alone any improvement on previous physical condition.

Interval training is a logical system of improving heart endurance by imposing greater demands through an increase in pace and the introduction of recovery period. More work can be done in a given period of time and it identifies more closely with the demands of the game. It is, therefore, an ideal form of training as the season approaches.

It also makes demands on anaerobic capacity, thus players are subjected to more specific conditioning in terms of the game.

Swedish physiologists suggest the following schedule which would appear to present the logical progression required:

1. Five minutes of warm-up, which includes easy running and simple limbering-up exercises—arm circling (backwards) movements, trunk twisting and circling, knee bending and stretching, and stretching in the lunge position.

2. Follow with five minutes of spurt training,
   (a) Running at top speed for 20–30 strides with
   (b) recovery between spurts.

3. Follow with 15–20 minutes of INTERVAL TRAINING based on
   (a) Runs at 80 per cent of top speed for bouts of two to four minutes with
   (b) rest of jog recovery of approximately same duration between runs.

As you improve in fitness you will undoubtedly increase the number of runs in your spurt training, and increase their length from 20 to 30 strides.

Progression can be implemented along the following lines in spurt training:

1st–3rd sessions	5×20 strides
4th session	$1 \times 30; 4 \times 20$ strides
5th session	$2 \times 30; 3 \times 20$ strides
6th session	$3 \times 30; 2 \times 20$ strides
7th session	4×30 strides
8th session	5×30 strides
9th session	6×30 in the 5 minutes

The interval training session will progress in terms of higher quality running during the running stages, i.e. a higher pace can be maintained in the later runs. A decrease in resting time can be introduced when aerobic fitness improves. The recovery heart rate can be a good indicator of when to start successive runs. Athletics coaches use a recovery heart rate of 120 as a threshold indicator. When the rate drops below 120 the next run is commenced. Players can use such a procedure as a guide for progression, and indeed as an indicator of improvement, for the resting period should shorten if the same running pace is maintained in workouts (a stop watch would help you to record this).

Fartlek running, or speed play, is a form of running over

natural surfaces—varied terrain of uphill, downhill, woodland, forest paths, grass tracks, the surrounds of golf courses etc. The runs feature a mixing of fast steady-pace running, sprinting, slow interval running, acceleration running uphill etc., which are meant to influence the different factors contributing to running endurance. Such runs are enjoyable and informal, but require a certain inner discipline to ensure that comparable efforts are made in successive runs. Cross-country running is also a suitable activity for building up endurance levels.

An interesting method of encouraging the heavier forward to engage in continuous running activity is to compare his speed per pound weight with his fellow players, a minimum distance of say two miles being accepted as being the running target. The player's time for running this distance is recorded in seconds and this score is divided by his bodyweight in pounds,

e.g. 14 minutes for 2 miles $= 840$ seconds
Bodyweight (14 st 8 lb) in pounds $= 204$ lb

$$\text{Speed/Pound} = \frac{840}{204} = 4 \cdot 1$$

In this way the score of the forward can be favourably compared with that of the half back or three-quarter.

Once the immediate pre-season training programme begins, players are subjected to intensive individual, unit and team skills training with the fitness emphasis being placed on anaerobic type running and modified circuit training. Such running programmes should be quantified to a certain extent, otherwise progression and overload principles cannot be applied. "Up the field", or "club type" training is typical of such running activities, and is a good example of how the running demands of the game can be simulated. It will be remembered that players are expected to cover anything between 4,000 and 6,000 yards in a game, and between one third and one half of which is done at speed. Therefore, a good objective in training would be to build up a series of fast runs to cover a total distance of 2,000 to 3,000 yards. We must further remember that such training is often done after other work has been completed in unit and team tactical training. This results in a total work output far in excess of that required in the game—which, of course, is necessary.

Goal line to 25-yard line   × 4 ⎫
   walk/jog back   ⎪
Goal line to halfway line   × 3 ⎬   Approximately 500 yards
   walk/jog back   ⎪   of fast running × 3
Goal line to other 25-yard line × 2 ⎪   = 1,500 yards
   walk/jog back   ⎪
Goal line to goal line   × 1 ⎭

The runs are flat-out sprints so we get in effect a programme of *repetition sprints* increasing on a pyramid progression.

The quantity of quality running is controlled, and progression takes the form of increasing the number of sets, i.e. adding a further block of 500 yards. 2,500 yards of such repetition sprinting could be considered an acceptable maximum training objective for speed endurance training.

These runs could also be done in blocks of 25×12; 55×9; 85×6; 110×3 increasing to 25×16 etc.

Repetition sprinting carried out under competitive conditions and incorporating a one to two work/rest ratio can also be done in the following manner (shuttle sprints).

Two players, one with a ball, stand on the goal line while the third member of the trio is on the 22-metre line. On a command, the player with the ball runs to his partner on the 22, and on handing the ball to him, calls out "One", his partner runs back to goal line and hands to the third member of the team, calling out "Two" as he does so. The exercise continues for the prescribed time—30 seconds. The total score of runs is noted. A rest of 30 seconds is given, and the sprints begin again.

Progression and overload can be applied through

(a) increasing the work time, i.e. 30 seconds to 60 seconds,

(b) increasing the number of repetitions i.e. 5 × 30 seconds,

8 × 30 seconds,

(c) reducing rest period,

(d) increasing distance of run.

If the same partners are used, this form of training can offer a wonderful opportunity to see if fitness improves, in that the total number of sprints performed by the trio in one minute could be recorded at the beginning of August and checked again at various intervals throughout the season. In order to provide an opportunity for training effect to reveal itself, the distance run should be from goal line to halfway line. No ball should be used in a testing situation—it may be dropped and thus affect the true training improvement.

Continuous relay running, paarlauf relays and long shuttle runs are other forms of training which can control the work/rest ratios we require to enforce.

Figs. 24 to 27 show some examples of continuous relays. In Fig. 24 X runs with ball and hands to X2, X2 to X3 etc. Player after handing over the ball takes up the position of player he replaces, i.e. X1 takes X2's place. The relay continues for five to ten minutes; the number of circuits is recorded; and as fitness increases so should the distance run. In order to progress, increase the work time.

Paarlauf (pair running) is a more demanding form of training. In Fig. 25 X1 starts at the halfway line, he runs around half the pitch and hands ball to X2. After handing over the ball he jogs to his original starting position. X2 hands him the ball and he jogs to his original position and so on. It can be a competitive activity because more than one pair can run at a time, however, because of the intensity of work it must be of shorter duration than the first relay.

Shuttle running is a good form of speed endurance training but the runs need to be in the order of 25–35 seconds. Fig. 26 shows

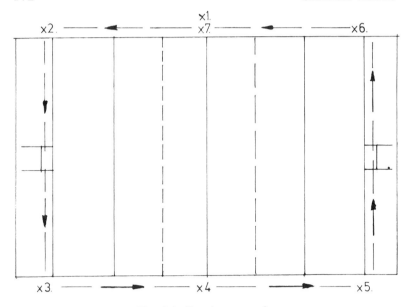

Fig. 24. Continuous relay.

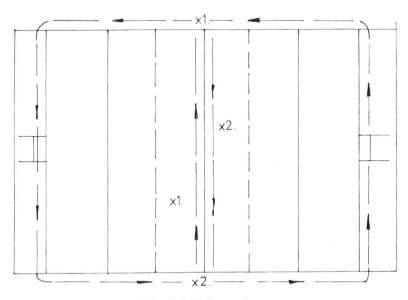

Fig. 25. Pair running.

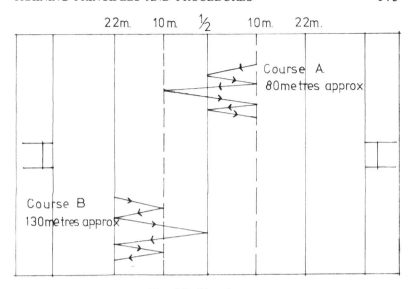

Fig. 26. Shuttle runs.

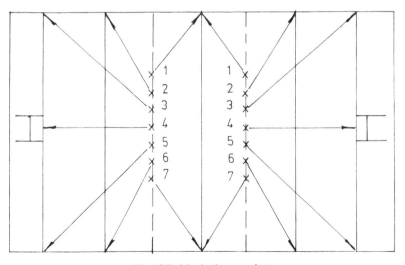

Fig. 27. Variation sprints.

two courses, A and B. Rest intervals approximating to those of
the game, 20–40 seconds, should be used, but obviously longer
rest intervals would need to be used for Course B than for Course
A. If a work/rest ratio of one to two is used many more runs can
be performed.

Sprints using a variety of distances can also be used to improve
anaerobic capacity. Fig. 27 provides an example. On a signal X1,
2, 3 etc. sprint to the perimeter of the pitch and then jog back. X1
moving to X2's starting position etc. The signal is given every 30
seconds so that there is a varying rest/work interval.

Another method is to use a rectangle such as that formed by
half a pitch. A sprint is made down one side of the rectangle
followed by a jog around the other three sides. Then sprint down
two sides and jog two; sprint three, jog one, followed immediately
by sprinting down four sides. A short rest, then repeat. Progression again is by increased repetition and decreased rest periods.

Speed

Training of the correct emphasis can improve innate speed but
we must remember that the natural carthorse will never be able to
compete with the natural racehorse in terms of pure speed. As I
have already mentioned the ability to improve upon leg speed is
much in doubt. The greatest area of improvement will come from
trying to increase stride length through the application of explosive power. This is the ability to exert maximum force in a
minimum of time and is vital to the development of acceleration
speed. The quality of power is probably Rugby football's most
sought-after fitness element. Where the resistance is great, for
instance on a heavy ground, strength of leg is particularly important, for this has the greater influence on speed. Research has
shown that top speed is not attained until after 30 metres
(Japanese study) and 50 metres (French study) have been reached.
Such work further relates to the value of strength to speed. In
Rugby, where the effective running distance probably varies between 10 and 40 yards it is strength-orientated speed that we

require most. This is achieved through increasing strength of the leg in the driving phase (leg extension), improving flexibility of the hip and using running drills to improve co-ordination.

Hopping, bounding (single and double leg bounds) and giant stride runs with pronounced body lean, over distances ranging from 22 metres to the full length of the football pitch, are considered by Russian coaches to be absolutely essential for developing explosive strength, or, as Frank Dick calls it, "elastic" strength. This kind of training is easily done by the Rugby player, is easily measured on the field and can be adjusted to provide overload principles. Repetition hops (each leg in turn) over 22 metres can be built up from 3×22 m, 6×22 m, then 4×50 m, 6×50 m, to 6×60 m, thereby increasing the distance hopped. Giant strides can be used in the same way but over longer distances. Improvement in elastic strength can be shown simply by timing how long it takes to hop a fixed distance or by recording the vertical jump (see measurement chapter).

Resistance running is another form of training which can be practised by running repeatedly a fixed number of strides up an incline (not too steep, otherwise the running form becomes decidedly different), with the object of trying to cover a greater distance on each run through a concentrated drive on the rear leg, good front leg lift and backward drive of the arm. Other forms of resistance running include pulling tyres (or a partner) over a fixed distance, the exercise to be repeated six to ten times, increasing by sets to three sets of ten (30 seconds between runs and three to four minutes between sets). Overload can again be applied through adding an additional tyre to the load or increasing the distance run.

It is important to realise that when one is concentrating on the development of pure speed one should take long rests to ensure total recovery between runs. Where speed endurance is the objective then limited rest periods are introduced.

Strengthening work also features the inclusion of special leg flexion exercises in the weight-training schedules, particularly during the close season. As the season approaches, and during the competition season, players should employ power-building principles where the load is reduced and repetitions are increased, the whole exercise being executed at speed.

Strength

I have long been an advocate of strength training for Rugby football. The game demands strength in so many of its facets—scrummaging, mauling, making tackles etc.—and no player can be too strong. In my experience the reverse applies, and many players are nowhere near strong enough. Sometimes on testing the leg power of young locks I have found that some of them can only manage a vertical jump of 17 inches. How can they possibly be line-out jumpers? Players in the Welsh National Squad with a weight in excess of 16 stone can manage jumps of 26 to 27 inches. The kind of strength required will, of course, vary according to position. Backs and back-row forwards will require more power-endurance-type strength, whereas the tight forward can benefit from greater raw strength. However, it would be safe to assume that what is generally required is "dynamic" strength, i.e. that strength which can be repeatedly applied at speed. It is this quality with which we are ultimately concerned.

In order to develop strength we have to induce increased tension in the muscle, a principle known as "overload". This must be progressively applied in order to obtain optimal strength development. Dynamic tension, gymnastics, sandhill running, mountain runs, weight lifting, heavy work, weight training and pulling etc., all have been suggested as being good systems for acquiring greater strength. They all do improve strength but some of them have limitations for progressive strength development. Bearing such limitations in mind I have no doubt that weight training correctly performed and properly administered is the most effective method of developing dynamic strength for Rugby football.

Points in favour of weight training are that it can be done at home, is not influenced by weather, can be adapted to the individual, does not require a large training area, can be used to develop specific areas of the body, allows for the application of flexible strength training systems and most importantly can easily use the overload principle.

There are many and varied systems of working with weights. In the past weight training was thought to "slow you down and make you muscle-bound". Contrary to these beliefs research has shown that co-ordination, mobility, flexibility and speed have been improved as a result of weight training. The Rugby player can utilise this experience and derive much benefit, provided certain fundamental principles are observed.

BASIC PRINCIPLES OF WEIGHT TRAINING

1. Weight training must *follow a plan* allowing progression.
2. The *load* must be at least greater than one third of maximum strength exertion to ensure strength development. A basic principle here is the greater the load, the greater the strength development.
3. Progression can be implemented through increasing load or the number of the times a movement is repeated (*repetitions*). These repetitions are usually grouped into sets, e.g. three sets of ten repetitions.
4. Exercise every other day (three times per week), thus allowing a day for recovery.
5. Warm up thoroughly before lifting weights.
6. Exercise large muscles of body and upper legs first, exercising smaller muscles later.
7. Stop exercising when movements cannot be performed correctly (straining to complete sets is to be avoided at all costs).
8. Do not exercise similar muscle groups consecutively.
9. When lifting weights from floor, keep back straight, body balanced with feet placed flat, normally eight to twelve inches apart, and head up.

10. Breathe freely throughout all movement (some authorities recommend inhaling on the initial effort, slight holding of breath during exertion against weight, exhaling on return to start position).

11. Ensure that all locking nuts are firmly secured.

Progressive weight training is based principally upon the theory that the intensity of work should be gradually increased. For the development of raw strength, heavy loads (90 per cent of maximum) and low repetitions (five to six) are recommended, but for muscular endurance medium to light loads (40–70 per cent) with higher repetitions (8–12) are advised. Power development for skill sports appears to involve a combination of the endurance principle for load (30–60 per cent) and high repetitions (10–25) coupled with the additional factor of speed—the movements performed as fast as possible. When increased tension is induced through the application of very fast repetitions, some authorities recommend that a weight which can be lifted for ten repetitions only (approximately 70 per cent of maximum load) should be used. This latter approach is the basis of the power schedule suggested below.

WEIGHT TRAINING FOR RUGBY FOOTBALL

Any additional strength that a player acquires should contribute to his physical output during the game. Present playing trends emphasise speed and power, so players should be primarily concerned with the development of these particular physical characteristics. The two schedules offered below have been designed with this purpose in mind. The basic strength schedule is presented as an introduction to strength and endurance development for those players not accustomed to weight training. The power weight-training schedule is more specific to game requirements, exercises muscle groups used continuously in the game, and is sufficiently taxing in effort for those players who are experienced in handling weights.

BASIC STRENGTH TRAINING SCHEDULE

Load—a weight that can be moved correctly for 8 repetitions.
Repetitions—8 increasing gradually to 12.
Sets—2 sets of 8 repetitions building up to 2 sets of 12.

Progression is based on building up the number of repetitions first, then increasing the load. After 2 sets of 12 repetitions can be executed correctly in good form, then one should readjust the load until only eight repetitions can be performed. This increased load will then form the starting weight for a further build-up to 12 repetitions as before.

The basic introductory schedule should be followed for approximately six to ten weeks. Poundages will increase rapidly at first, due to increased familiarity with the exercises and initial strength gains. Exercise three times per week OUT-OF-SEASON, reducing to twice or more per week during the season (avoiding training the day before a match).

WARM-UP

Physiologists have varied opinions on the beneficial effect of warm-up. Some suggest that it improves physiological efficiency, while others suggest that the benefit is purely psychological. Nevertheless, it is recommended that a non-specific warm-up routine (about ten mintes) of free standing exercises involving stretching, twisting, flexing and extending movements be performed prior to handling weights. Some short cardio-respiratory stimulating exercises should also be included. Coaches are familiar with such exercises, but a sample of some suitable exercises is presented as a guide.

This is followed by specific warm-up exercises using medium weights.

Warm-up exercises: Arm circling backwards × 10
Trunk circling × 10 (5 each side)
Astride Jumps × 50

Trunk flexion—alternate leg × 10
Lunge sit × 5 (each leg)
Burpees × 20

Specific Warm-Up (with weights)—barbell 50–60 pounds:
(a) Power Clean 12 × 2
(b) High Pull Ups 12 × 2
(c) Crouch to stand × 5
   Thigh rest to clean position × 5
   Press × 5 (2 sets)

BASIC SCHEDULE

Exercise	Body region exercised
1. Bicep Curl	Front of upper arm, forearm and wrist
2. Trunk Curl (with or without inclined bench)	Front of trunk (Abdominals)
3. Power Clean	Leg, back, shoulders
4. Parallel Squat	Thighs and buttocks
5. Standing or Seated Press	Shoulders and back of upper arms
6. Back extension	Lower and upper back
7. Bent over Rowing	Back of shoulders, upper arms and lower back

After the basic schedule has been followed for six to ten weeks, the player can then progress to a more advanced strength schedule of exercises which are selected to satisfy his own needs:

This procedure should be approached in the following manner:

(a) analyse requirements of player's position and determine the contributory movements to effective play;
(b) select exercises which work the muscles that cause the movements;

(c) determine maximum amount of weight that can be lifted for one repetition in each exercise, and use 70–80 per cent of this maximum weight;

(d) perform at least three sets of each exercise doing as many repetitions as possible in each set. If more than eight can be performed then the load is too light (some strength athletes perform as many as 5–15 sets with loads of 80–90 per cent of maximum doing only two to three repetitions). Tight forwards are advised to adjust the load close to 80–90 per cent of maximum and complete sets of five repetitions building up to four or five sets, since their requirement is principally one of raw pushing and support strength;

(e) rest two to three minutes between sets;

(f) work out on alternate days. During the playing season it is essential to work out at least once per week in order to maintain strength levels.

Strength, we must remember, in addition to being an important trait in itself, also influences the other performance traits of power, muscular endurance, agility and running speed, quite markedly. The strength/endurance relationship can be illustrated as follows:

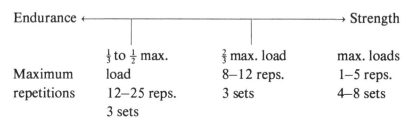

Endurance ←			→ Strength
Maximum repetitions	$\frac{1}{3}$ to $\frac{1}{2}$ max. load 12–25 reps. 3 sets	$\frac{2}{3}$ max. load 8–12 reps. 3 sets	max. loads 1–5 reps. 4–8 sets

Power

(Strength orientated)

Recent research has shown that if power is the component to be developed, then heavy weight training may not be the most suitable form of training for playing field games. Japanese physiologists suggest that weights between 30 and 60 per cent of maximum poundages be utilised for training purposes, the training effect being specific in its own direction, i.e. use 30 per cent for speed emphasis and 60 per cent for the strength gain.

Rugby players then, after working on the basic schedule for ten weeks, should apply power training principles. It would be appropriate to work more towards the strength aspect of the "Force-velocity curve" during the off season period May–August, implementing 60–70 per cent of maximum poundage. As the season gradually gets under way, the load can be reduced until 35–40 per cent maximum load is used for training. The speed of the movements and number of repetitions should increase accordingly.

It is important when using this principle to make a careful note of progression. After the load has been determined, the time it takes to perform the fixed number of repetitions (ten) should be recorded, e.g., ten seconds. Training should aim towards reducing this time—say to six seconds. When the time taken to perform the ten repetitions no longer improves, an attempt is made to ascertain a new maximum poundage for the exercise. Once this has been established training continues with the new load as before.

As the season approaches and lighter loads are handled the repetitions should be increased in the following manner— 15 repetitions for 60 per cent, 20 repetitions for 45–50 per cent, 25 repetitions for 35–40 per cent of maximum loads.

Travers of St Luke's, Exeter, on the evidence of his research findings, suggests that a load of equivalent to two-thirds maximum be used for 12 repetitions, the aim being to reduce the time of executing the number of repetitions. This load is close to that suggested by Ikai for improving the strength aspect of the force–velocity curve. Progression in Travers' system is achieved differently. When the time for performing 12 repetitions cannot be improved any further, then an additional five repetitions is performed, the aim then being to reduce the time taken to perform 17 repetitions. Increments of five repetitions are suggested. He does, however, suggest that the ultimate number of repetitions performed should be related to the duration of non-stop activity in the sport in which one participates. In our case 30 seconds should be the ultimate time limit.

Such an approach offers an alternative means of building power. A change of system is often as good as a rest.

A specimen power training schedule is presented to illustrate some of the above points:

Load—the suggested percentage of maximum weight to be handled might vary for each exercise, since some of the muscle groups have more relative strength and endurance than others. The weight used is that which can be handled for ten repetitions (approximately 70 per cent of <u>maximum one repetition</u>).

Repetitions—ten executed in correct form at speed, the time to be recorded.

Objective—to reduce the time of performing ten repetitions until it can no longer be improved.

Warm Up—as before.

1. Power clean—load 70% × 10 reps.
2. Press seated—70% × 10.
3. Sit Ups (inclined bench if possible—Weight behind neck) 10 reps × 2 sets.
4. Bicep Curl (Cheat) 70% × 10.
5. Back extensions (hips supported on bench—weight behind neck) 10 × 2.
6. Half squat to sit (16-inch bench) 70% × 10.
7. Bench press 70% × 10.
8. Step up on bench (16 inch) 70% × 10.
   In this form of training it is safer to keep the working leg on the bench the whole time, so that it extends and flexes supporting the weight. Change legs after ten repetitions have been completed.

As adaptation takes place a second set of repetitions can be added, and the same principles of training utilised. Alternatively, a new load should be determined as strength levels will have increased.

Where time is a limiting factor in training, weight-training schedules are often curtailed and exercises reduced to three or four exercises only. In these cases, warm up should not be neglected, and sit-ups and back extensions could be included in this part of the training.

The following four exercises could present an acceptable abbreviated schedule for players:

1. Power clean.
2. Seated press two sets, with a third set of press behind neck.
3. Bicep (cheat) curl.
4. Half squat to sit—done quickly.

We are concerned with developing strength to play Rugby. There are other more specific and better ways of improving the other factors of endurance, running speed, agility, but we must not forget that strength is an important contributory factor.

Often players have no access to weight-training equipment. They can, however, make their own weight-training barbell by using piping and empty seven or ten-pound jam or canned potato tins, the type used at school or hospital canteens.

Do-it-yourself barbell.

Materials: 1-1½" diameter iron /steel piping 4'— 6" in length

4 × 6" nails

Concrete mix of 3 parts fine chipping, 2 parts sand

and 1 — 1½ parts cement.

2 old cans(7—10lbs jam tins or ½ gallon paint tins)

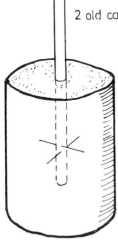

Directions: Drill two holes at right angles to each other one approx.

2" from the end of the bar and the other 4" from the end.
Insert the two 6"nails.

Stand one end in tin, pour in mixed concrete and allow to
stand for 3/4 days keeping bar vertical.

Repeat other end.

Approximate weight of completed bar 40 — 50lbs. Weigh
on bathroom scales to obtain correct weight.

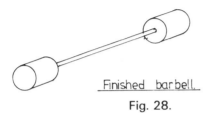

Finished barbell.

Fig. 28.

An exercise stool can easily be made out of half-inch plywood and three-quarter-inch chipboard as in Fig. 29.

By using the two pieces of home-made equipment illustrated above, a very effective home fitness strength/power/endurance schedule can be designed. The following is an illustration of what can be done:

Spend 3–5 minutes warming up using stretching and twisting movements, free standing arm exercises followed by stepping up and down on the bench (20 times each leg), some sit ups and burpees.

Schedule

1. Half squats to sit × 30 (barbell on shoulders), Figs. 30 and 30a. Follow with two sets doing as many as possible in 20 secs. 30 secs. between sets.
2. Seated press behind neck × 12, Figs. 31 and 31a. Follow with 2 sets of 10 secs.
3. Sit up—feet fixed under stool, body on floor, Figs. 32 and 32a. Hand behind neck. Sit up until elbows touch knees. 20 × 3. Follow with 2 sets of 10 secs.
4. Half squat clean and press, Figs. 33 and 33a. From half squat position, clean the bar while staying down, then stand and press overhead. Repeat × 12. Follow with sets of 10 secs.
5. Bicep curl × 12, Figs. 34 and 34a. Follow with 2 sets of 10 secs.
6. Bench step up, Figs. 35 and 35a. Weight on shoulders, step up on box with left leg, then with right, down with left, down with right. Repeat 30 times with left leg leading, then 30 times with right leg leading. Rest one minute. Repeat × 2.
7. Press-ups (feet on box, hands on floor) × 12, Figs. 36 and 36a. Follow with two sets of 10 secs.

An Exercise Stool.

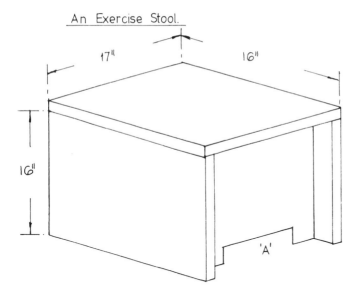

Top of box made of 3/4" chipboard — 17"×16"
Side panels are made of 1/2" plywood — 16"×15¼"
2 side panels are recessed 1½".

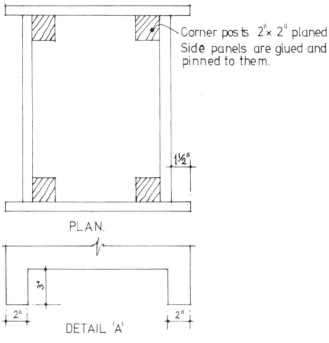

Corner posts 2"× 2" planed
Side panels are glued and
pinned to them.

PLAN.

DETAIL 'A'

Fig. 29.

Fig. 30.

Fig. 30a.

Fig. 31.

Fig. 31a.

Fig. 32.

Fig. 32a.

Fig. 33.

Fig. 33a.

Fig. 34.

Fig. 34a.

Fig. 35.

Fig. 35a.

8. Half–three-quarter squat, Figs. 37 and 37a. Start by sitting on box, weight on shoulders. Rise until a position is reached where the legs are only bent to about 135–140°, then lower. Lower to sit position (do not sit, only let backside touch box). Repeat fast × 30. Follow with two sets of 30 secs.

Progression in the above schedule can be obtained by increasing the working time of the timed second and third sets, e.g. progress by five second increments from 10–15–20–25–30. When two sets of 30 seconds of exercise can be performed, then add a third set. This schedule can prove to be very strenuous when executed in this way. Rest between exercises—two to three minutes.

FREE-STANDING EXERCISE SCHEDULES FOR DEVELOPING POWER

The following sequence of exercises suggested by the Scandinavian Trim programme seems to be admirably suited for the anaerobic-type training required for Rugby football, and is given here for your benefit:

1. Lie on the floor, face down, hands under shoulders. Keeping body straight raise yourself up on your arms until elbows are straight, then lower.
   Do as many press-ups as possible for 30 seconds. Rest 30 seconds. Repeat four times. Increase until eight sets can be done. (Vary distance between hands.)
2. Lie on your back. Raise upper body until vertical, turning to right as you do so, then next time straight up, third time to left etc. Repeat for 30 seconds. Rest 30 seconds. Repeat three times, progress to six sets.
3. Lie on stomach, arms at sides. Raise top half of body the first time turning to the left, the second time straight up and the third turning to the right. Continue for 30 seconds. Rest one minute. Repeat two times, progress to four sets.
4. Jump on the spot, keeping knees at 90° at the outset. After jumping, return directly to the flexed position and then jump again. Repeat for 20 seconds. Rest one minute. Repeat for 20 seconds. Progress until six sets of 20 seconds can be performed, then increase work time to 30 seconds and

gradually increase each set until six sets of 30 seconds are achieved.

Exercise three times a week pre-season and twice during the season—not on Fridays, the day before a game.

An additional general exercise could be inserted between exercise 2 and 3. This is:

Front support position (press-up position) keeping arms straight, sag at the hips, then lift hips and bring left foot forward to place between the hands then return. Sag again at hips and do likewise with right foot.

Repeat for 30 seconds. Rest 30 seconds. Increase from two sets to six sets.

The above schedules provide a form of strength endurance and speed endurance training. They are designed for home use, but of course can be used by whole teams provided clubs make their own equipment.

Circuit Training is a well established form of training designed to improve strength, muscular endurance, muscular power and cardio-respiratory (aerobic) endurance. The system is well known and needs no introduction here. Those players or coaches unfamiliar with the system should read *Circuit Training* by Morgan and Adamson, published by Bell, London. It is an excellent form of all-round training for playing-field games. Yet it can be modified a little to meet more specifically the demands of the game by setting individual loads of two-thirds maximum instead of the recognised half maximum load in order to influence more the strength level of development, an element we require greatly in Rugby football. Such adjustments are only applicable in individual designed circuits.

OUTDOOR FITNESS CIRCUIT

A proven method for improving general fitness along with building up muscular endurance, is that of "Target Training", a system of training promoted by E. S. Lewis, New Zealand. In British Columbia, so-called "Fitness Circuits" have been erected in some of their parks in order to promote "Community Health". These circuits appear to have been based upon target-training principles and are performed after preliminary warm-up runs to elevate heart rate to at least twice the resting pulse-rate level. Such circuits can be easily adapted to suit the *general* fitness require- ments of Rugby Football. An example of such an *adapted* "out- door circuit" is presented for your information.

These courses can also be used to encourage ordinary non-play- ing club members to keep fit and thereby establish "contact" with players, and even form play areas for those children who accom- pany their parents on match days. Modifications to some of the suggested exercises would need to be made in these cases. Target times indicating varying standards of fitness could be displayed to create further interest among players and non-players. The ex- ample below illustrates how such target times could be displayed.

Fitness Category	18–29 years	30–39 years	40–50+ years
Poor	More than 14 minutes	More than 14.30 minutes	More than 15.30 minutes
Fair	11–14.20 minutes	11.30–14.30 minutes	12.30–15.30 minutes
Good	9.30–11 minutes	10–11.30 minutes	11–12.30 minutes
Excellent	Less than 9.30 minutes	Less than 10 minutes	Less than 11 minutes

Figs. 38 to 41 give structural details of the various exercise sta- tions. Materials for construction can be obtained from local builders' merchants, and the items made at the club house. Kee Klamp Systems, Thornsett Road, London S.W.12. offer a convenient tubing and clamping system which can be easily assembled (like a (meccano set) to form many of the items shown. The Forestry

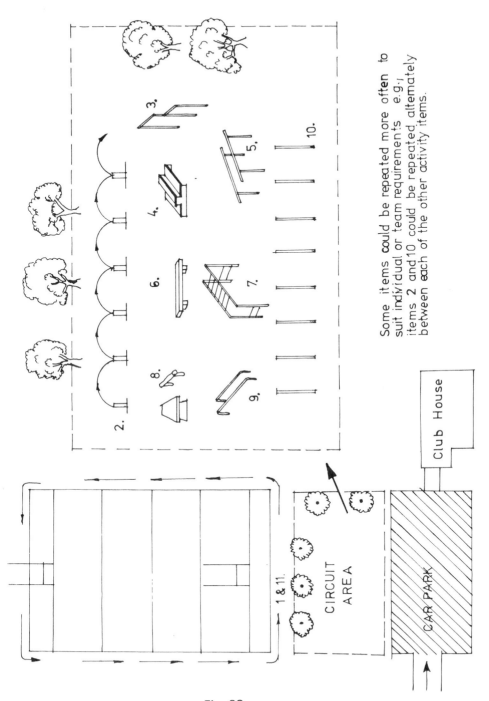

Some items could be repeated more often to suit individual or team requirements e.g. items 2 and 10 could be repeated alternately between each of the other activity items.

Fig. 38.

Outdoor Fitness Circuit

1. Run six laps of rugby pitch
    (approximately 1¼ miles)

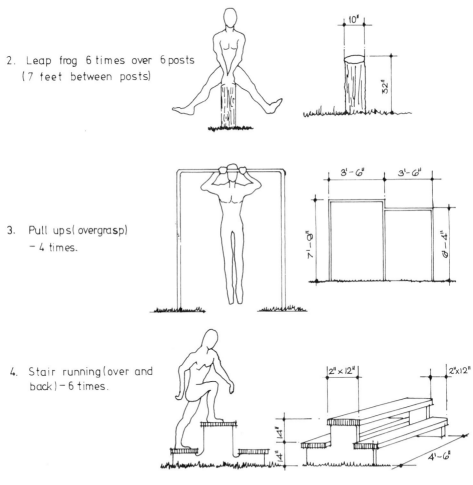

2. Leap frog 6 times over 6 posts
    (7 feet between posts)

3. Pull ups (overgrasp)
    – 4 times.

4. Stair running (over and
    back) – 6 times.

Fig. 39.

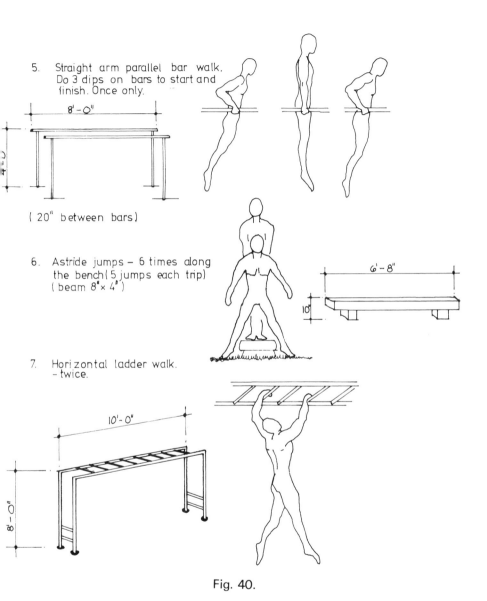

5. Straight arm parallel bar walk.
    Do 3 dips on bars to start and
    finish. Once only.

    8' - 0"

    (20" between bars)

6. Astride jumps – 6 times along
    the bench (5 jumps each trip)
    (beam 8" × 4")

    6' - 8"

    10"

7. Horizontal ladder walk.
    - twice.

    10' - 0"

    8' - 0"

Fig. 40.

8.   Bench sit ups — 10 times.

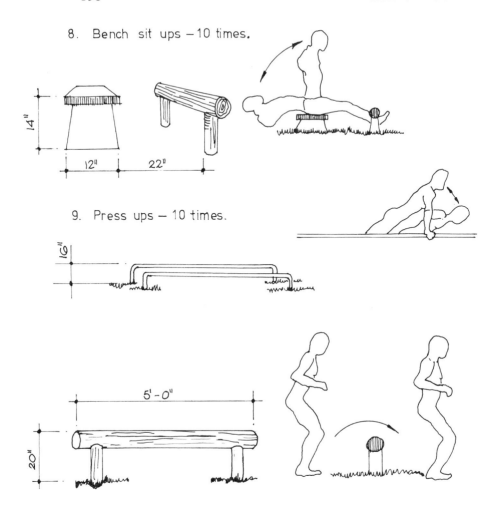

9.   Press ups — 10 times.

10.   Obstacle run with two-footed jumps
      over hurdles - 6 times.
      (6 hurdles, 10 feet between)

11.   Wind down with a 4 lap run.

*Note time of finishi

Fig. 41.

Commission supply suitable timber for many of the items and can also supply pine needles, sawdust, chopped bark etc. to form a springy base at some of the exercise stations. Pine trees planted at suitable sites on the perimeter and within the exercise area can help to create a natural and pleasing setting for the circuit. Many years ago I persuaded the Moseley club, I was a member at the time, to erect an outdoor circuit. It was simple but was well used. Eventually, however, the area was required for car parking. Such is progress!

TEAM CONDITIONING METHODS

Although it is primarily the responsibility of the player to present himself to team training session in a fit enough condition to accept any form of training that the coach demands of him, I feel that at least ten minutes should be spent at the end of training sessions for specific team conditioning, based on short-interval type work, such as those suggested below, designed to make excessive demands upon the anaerobic processes. A wind-down session of two or three minutes' easy running should *always* follow such sessions.

1. *Short-Interval Circuit Training* Standard circuit-type activities performed for 20 to 30 seconds only, as fast as possible, a maximum effort being made at each exercise station. Introduce with a work/rest ratio of one to two.

Progression can be implemented through

(a) an increase in exercise time up to a 40 seconds maximum;
(b) reduction of rest phase to a work/rest ratio of one to one;
(c) introduction of a second circuit after a one to two minute rest between circuits;
(d) introduction of a third circuit.

Home-made weights and stools are very suitable for use in this type of work.

2. *Short-Interval Circuit with shuttle runs* As in 1, but introduce 15–20 yard shuttle runs between each standard exercise.

An Interval Run Circuit

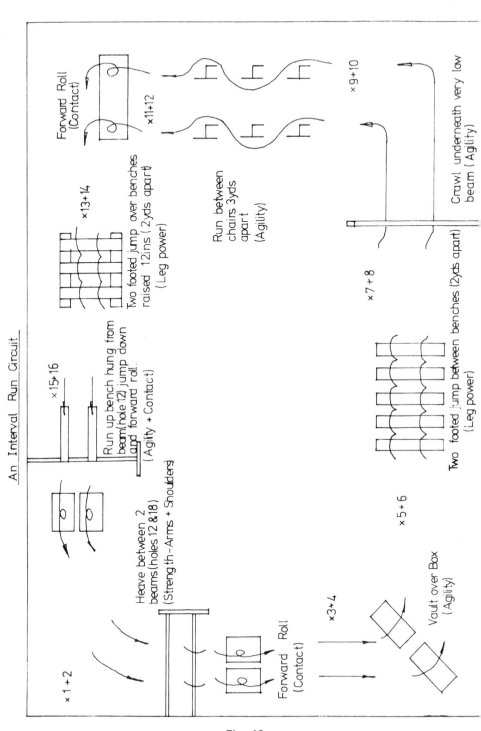

Fig. 42.

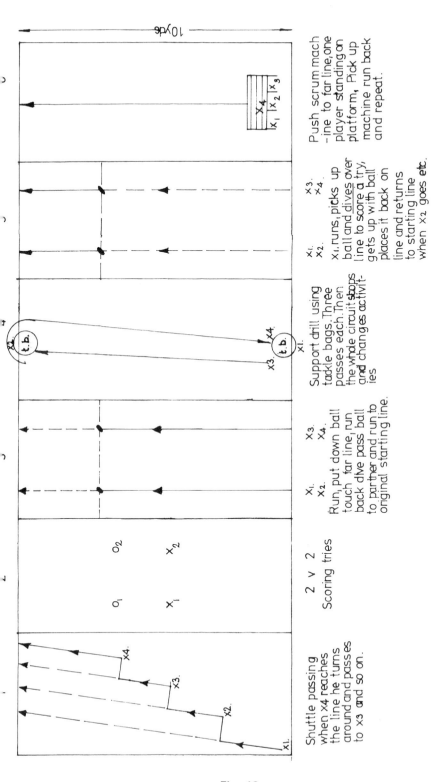

10 yd.

Shuttle passing when x4 reaches the line he turns around and passes to x3 and so on.

2 v 2 Scoring tries

x1. x3.
x2. x4.

Run, put down ball touch far line, run back dive pass ball to partner and run to original starting line.

Support drill using tackle bags. Three passes each. Then the whole circuit stops and changes activit-ies

x1. x3.
x2. x4.

x1. runs, picks up ball and dives over line to score a try, gets up with ball places it back on line and returns to starting line when x2 goes etc.

Push scrum mach -ine to far line, one player standing on platform, Pick up machine run back and repeat.

A Specific Short Interval Circuit.

Fig. 43.

3. *Interval Run Circuits (over obstacles)* Players are required to run in groups over a continuous obstacle course (Fig. 42) for periods ranging from 20 seconds to one minute. While one group runs, the other, or others, rest. Thus a work/rest ratio of one to two or one to one can be achieved as above. This can best be done by organising young players into three or two groups respectively. Stagger their starting positions.

Progression can be obtained through

(a) increasing work time;
(b) increasing number of runs;
(c) reducing rest time;
(d) setting a more difficult course, including contact on the ground through the introduction of rolls.

These can be organised indoors or outdoors. Use spectator railings, steps, chairs, flag posts etc.

4. *Specific Short-Interval Circuits* Similar to short-interval type circuits but with game type skills and techniques substituted in lieu of standard exercises. See diagram.

5. *"Up the pitch" running activity.*

6. *Intensive relay-type activities* e.g. shuttle relays where teams of three try to make maximum number of shuttles over 25 yards in one minute. With rest periods of 30 seconds between work stints (within the one-minute stint a work/rest ratio of one to two is obtained) a series of five to six runs can be achieved with the group trying to improve their score during the first three runs and maintain it during the latter three runs.

In recent years the search for fitness has been based on increasingly scientific principles, as I hope the preceding chapters will have indicated. Previously fitness was largely based on empirical knowledge and on "hit or miss" methods. Nowadays the demands on players are so great and the fitness requirements of the game so diverse that we cannot afford to spend training time on methods which do not pay dividends. We must therefore be sure that whatever training systems are used do, in fact, produce higher fitness levels. The only objective way to do this is to try, by administering certain selected tests to players, to measure the qualities which I have previously discussed as fitness components. By retesting at periodic intervals, we should be able to see if progress is being made, and also be able to compare results with other players of a similar standard.

Furthermore, by testing players of an accepted high playing standard we can to some extent see what fitness values are desirable. Sometimes of course even players of international standing are deficient in some physical qualities, but at least testing such players helps us to put fitness values into perspective. A well organised testing programme on a regular basis has much to commend it. Apart from providing a yardstick by which training systems can be assessed, it also pin-points strengths and weaknesses in individual players. Another important bonus is the incentive it gives to players, for it motivates them to do well.

For the past nine years we have carried out a fairly simple testing programme on players' courses which we arrange as part of our summer programme in Aberystwyth. This work has been supervised by Gwyn Evans, one of our Staff Coaches and a member of the Physical Education Department in the University there. Gwyn has a particular interest in conditioning, and as I stated in my foreword the entire fitness section in this book is based on his material and experience. As a result of the testing programmes, we have built up a considerable amount of data on the fitness levels of young Welsh players. This gives a good indication to aspiring young players of the fitness levels for which they should be aiming. Gwyn Evans has also tested many senior club players and the scores for these and the young players are given for information and interest.

What then of the tests themselves? We have tried to devise a battery of tests considered appropriate to testing the kind of fitness required in Rugby football. Most of the tests can be carried out with little special equipment that is not found in the ordinary school gymnasium. A few require more sophisticated apparatus, such as grip and back/leg dynamometers, but even these probably could be borrowed from a university or college physical education department. The tests are appended so that coaches and players can experiment and see how they measure up to the demands of the game.

If tests are to be used then they must be conducted properly and in the right kind of atmosphere, otherwise the whole exercise becomes a waste of time. We must also exercise caution in the interpretation of results. The overriding aim of the Rugby player to improve skill and fitness is only a means to an end. It would be a great error of judgement to assume we could select a team on the evidence of fitness levels. They do, however, provide a useful measure of capacity both for coach and player.

For those intending to use tests there are some pertinent points which need to be made about measurement.

(a) Tests should be applied strictly to the method laid down and preferably at the same place and time on each occasion.
(b) The same person or persons should administer the test, using the same equipment each time, e.g. same stopwatch used by same person.

(c) Players should be motivated to do their best each time tested.

(d) Players should not have been engaged in a hard game or heavy physical training the day before testing.

(e) Players should undergo a light warm-up just prior to testing.

If the above suggestions are followed they will help to standardise procedures and make the results much more valid. Retesting at various times, e.g. June, September, December and March, will enable checks to be made on fitness levels. Another factor too is that they can be used as a guide to determine whether an injured player is fit enough to return to the game.

TESTS FOR RUGBY FITNESS

1. (a) Floor Push-Ups	Muscular Endurance
or (b) Parallel Bar Dips	(Arms and Shoulders)
2. Vertical Jump	Muscular Power
3. Shuttle Run	Muscular Power (Anaerobic energy),
(5 × 20 yards)	Agility and Speed
4. Leg Lifts in 30 seconds	Trunk strength
5. Pull-Ups	Muscular Endurance
	(Arms and Shoulders)
6. 600 yards Run	Speed Endurance
	(55% anaerobic/45% aerobic)
7. Arm Strength Index	Upper Body Strength in relation to
	body weight and height
8. Grip Strength	Hand, Forearm and General Strength
	indicator
9. Back lift	Lumbar strength
10. 12 minute Cooper Run	Aerobic Fitness

Other tests, of course, could be devised which would test more specifically particular aspects of Rugby fitness. For instance, Peter Duggan, a WRU Senior Coach at Penglais Comprehensive

School, Aberystwyth, designed a one-man scrummage machine to test scrummaging power. This was part of his study while at University College of Wales, Aberystwyth. The machine utilises a Salter Spring Scale Balance, and one feature which emerged was that maximum pushing power was obtained with leg flexion angle of 165°. Construction details of this machine can be obtained from the designer.

The suggested tests should be performed in the order given, so that generation of muscular fatigue is avoided, particularly so in the bar dip and pull-up test where a minimum period of ten minutes should separate the tests. When the grip- and back-lift test are included they should follow the pull-up test; the back-lift test being applied first, followed by the grip test, then the 600 yard run. The Arm Strength Index is not a test, but merely a score compiled from the raw scores obtained from bar dips and pull-ups. The 12-minute run should be performed on another day.

TESTING PROCEDURES

Most of the tests will be familiar to those who have been involved in physical activity. They are, with the exception of the push-up test, well described in *An Introduction to Tests and Measurements in Physical Education* by Campbell and Tucker, published by Bell in 1967.

1a. Floor push-ups

These are old friends to the physical trainer. They are subject to considerable variation in performance and are not reliable as a test unless strict conditions are enforced to standardise the test.

The body should be in the front support position, hands between shoulders, arms straight. The body is lowered until the chest touches the floor, arms are then immediately straightened. There must be a straight body position throughout and only hands and feet (and chest in the lowered position) make contact with the floor. One point is given each time the arms are straightened. No points are given for those occasions when the above conditions are not met.

1b. Parallel Bar Dips

These have a higher reliability than push-ups, but another reason in favour of this test is that Roger's formula can be used to

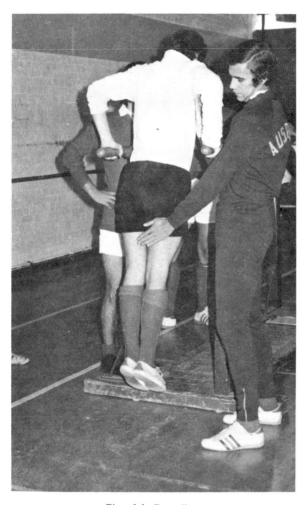

Fig. 44. Bar dips.

Fig. 45a. Vertical jump.

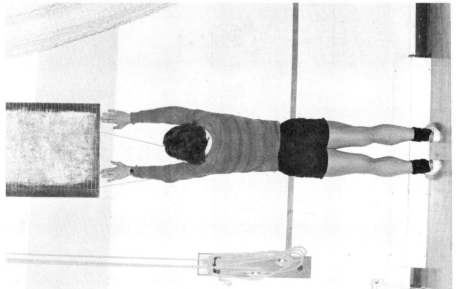

Fig. 45. Vertical jump.

compute Arm Strength Index. If parallel bars are not available they can be improvised using scaffolding pipes etc.

The body should be supported on straight arms. Attaining this position counts as one. Lower the body until the elbows are at right angles and push back to straight arms. This counts as two. Repeat until the movement cannot be continued. Swinging etc. is not allowed. If the straight position or right-angle position is not reached, half points can be given up to four half points (Fig. 44).

2. Vertical jump

This is a good indication of muscular power. Stand underneath a vertical jump board (Fig. 45). Stretch both arms upwards and adjust the board so that fingers just touch the bottom of the board. Turn sideways and stand slightly away from the board. Wet tips of the fingers of the right hand. Jump vertically and make a mark on the board (Fig. 45a). Three attempts are allowed and highest score is recorded. "Bouncing" prior to take-off is not allowed.

3. Shuttle Run

As advocated by Fleishman, requires a player to run a distance of 100 yards in five 20-yard continuous sprints. The best surface for the test is wood, concrete or macadam. Mark the distance with two lines 20 yards apart. One foot only needs to cross the line before the turn is made. The better time of two runs is recorded (Fig. 46).

4. Leg Lifts

These are again advocated by Fleishman, who found them a good single measure of trunk strength. Players should work in threes. One lies on his back with his hands behind his neck. He attempts to raise his straight legs at right angles to the floor as many times as possible in 30 seconds. One player holds down the player being tested by pressing his elbows to the floor and the other acts as a "counter" and ensures that the legs are raised to the proper position. "Bouncing" with the heels is not allowed.

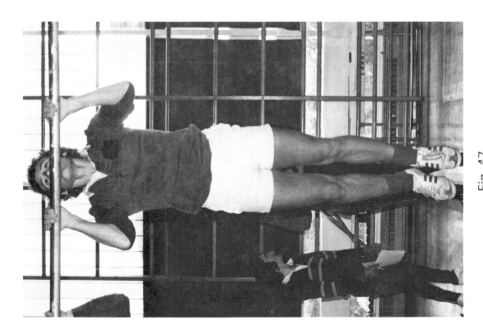

Fig. 47

Fig. 46

5. Pull-Ups

These are best performed on a bar two inches in diameter and at such a height as to allow the tallest player to hang *overgrasp* with his feet clear of the ground. Arms should be straight and shoulder width apart. Pull up until the chin is level with the top of the bar, lower to straight arms. Count the number of "chins". Swinging etc. is not allowed but a maximum of four half points can be given for incomplete efforts (Fig. 47).

6. 600 yard Run

This is simply a test of running this distance in the shortest possible time. The perimeter of the Rugby field can be used. The test is best done in groups. An easy way is to pair off players so that one records the time of the other, then vice versa. An accurate enough gauge is obtained if the timer calls out the time and resting partner notes when his running partner crosses the finishing line.

7. Arm Strength Index

This is determined by noting the number of pull-ups and bar dips recorded. Arm strength is then calculated according to the formula

$$\text{(Pull ups + Bar dips)} \times \left(\frac{W}{10} + H - 60 \right)$$

Where W = weight in pounds and H = height in inches.
Fractions are corrected to the nearest whole numbers.

The advantage of using an Arm Strength Score lies in the fact that the height and weight of the individual are taken into account. This is important in Rugby, where there are often huge differences in size between backs and forwards.

8. Grip Test

This is done by using the dominant hand. It can only be done using a hand dynamometer. The scores achieved in the norms

Fig. 48. Back lift.

given in the accompanying tables were achieved using a
Loughborough Triple Thrust Dynamometer, and comparisons
with scores made on other makes would be invidious. Two trials
are allowed, the arm or hand should not touch the body and the
better score is recorded in pounds.

9. Back Lift

This requires a back/leg dynamometer which are supplied by
Niasen Co., Brentwood, Essex. Two trials are allowed and the

better score recorded in pounds. No details of the test are given because I feel that the person administering this test should seek specialist advice before he does attempt it (Fig. 48).

10. 12-minute Run

This has recently been popularised in the Sunday Press. The test was devised by Kenneth Cooper of "Aerobics" fame. It is simply a matter of recording the distance run in 12 minutes, and again the Rugby Field can be used as a guide. The result is recorded in yards.

The whole testing programme, excluding that of the 12-minute Run, which should be done on another day, could through good organisation accommodate 30 players within an hour and a half. Testing time can be reduced if a team of helpers can be persuaded to supervise the tests. The testing session would be a good workout if players were well motivated during the tests. We do not have sufficient data yet to give valid norms and therefore this test is not included in the fitness tables.

INDIVIDUAL ASSESSMENT

Tables are appended which give indications of fitness levels of Welsh Players. Each individual can then assess his own fitness relative to the norms established in the Tables. A norm is merely a standard point of reference by which comparisons can be made. To register scores in terms of percentiles, merely locate the raw score and then read across to the percentile score column on the left. A percentile score of 90 means that a player scores better than 90 per cent of all players tested.

TABLE I
Physical Fitness Profile of Adult Welsh Rugby Players—Forwards and Backs

Classification	Percentile score	Bar[1] dips	Pull[2] up	Arm[3] strength	Vertical[4] jump	Shuttle[5] run	Leg[6] lifts	Grip[7] strength	Back[8] lift	600 yard[9] run
		No.	*No.*	*Score*	*In.*	*Secs.*	*No.*	*lb.*	*lb.*	*Secs.*
Excellent	100	35	14	1376	28·50	17·3	30	200	720	75
	95	26	12	975	27·25	17·7	28	184	658	84
	90	24	11	883	26·50	18·0	27	166	630	88
Very good	85	22	10	835	26·00	18·3	27	158	602	89
	80	21	9½	782	25·75	18·5	26	152	583	90
	75	20	8½	763	25·25	18·7	26	149	560	92
Good	70	19	8	729	25·00	18·8	25	145	551	93
	65	18	7½	711	24·50	19·0	25	145	541	94
	60	17	7	664	24·25	19·1	24	144	532	95
Average	55	16½	6½	618	24·00	19·3	24	140	520	95
	50	15½	6	606	23·50	19·4	24	139	506	97
	45	15	5½	582	23·00	19·6	23	135	501	99
Fair	40	14	5½	557	22·50	19·7	23	133	495	100
	35	13	5	520	22·25	19·8	23	126	489	100
	30	12½	4½	499	21·75	20·0	22	122	477	102
Poor	25	11½	4½	490	21·25	20·1	22	117	470	103
	20	11	4	461	21·00	20·3	21	114	453	105
	15	10	3½	439	20·50	20·4	21	110	428	105
Very Poor	10	9	2½	404	19·75	20·7	20	107	402	108
	5	6½	1½	300	18·75	21·3	19	101	380	114
	0	5	0	208	17·00	22·2	16	90	315	120
Range =	0 and 100th Percentile Scores									
Mean =		16·01	6·412	632·3	23·09	19·38	23·74	136·7	515·2	97·48
Standard Devn. =		6·185	3·072	217·4	2·54	0·959	2·909	23·59	81·59	8·582
No. of subjects =		91	91	91	118	118	118	118	90	76
Mean Age =	25·06 years (SD = 4·148)									

Mean Weight = 183·1 lb. (SD = 23·26) Mean Height = 70·76 ins. (SD = 2·726)

[1] Rogers' SI
[2] Rogers' SI
[3] Rogers' Index (Pull Up + Back Up) [Wt (lb.) + Ht (ins.) · 60]
[4] Jump and Reach (Morgan and Adamson)
[5] Fleishman (5 × 20 yards)
[6] Fleishman (in 30 secs.)
[7] Dominant Hand (Loughborough Triple Thrust Grip Dynamometer)
[8] Rank Dynamometer (Salter Scale)

TABLE II
Physical Fitness Profile Record of Welsh Youth Rugby Players—Forwards: 15–17 years

Classification	Percentile score	Bar[1] dips	Pull[2] up	Arm[3] strength	Vertical[4] jump	Shuttle[5] run	Leg[6] lifts	Grip[7] strength	Back[8] lift	600 yards[9] run
		No.	*No.*	*Score*	*In.*	*Secs.*	*No.*	*lb.*	*lb.*	*Secs.*
Excellent	100	23	16	884	30·00	18·0	27	170	580	85
	95	14½	11	805	27·00	18·6	25	146	537	93
	90	16	10	574	25·50	18·9	24	137	513	95
Very good	85	14½	9½	550	24·00	19·1	24	135	497	96
	80	13½	8½	518	23·25	19·3	22	131	485	97
	75	12½	8	501	22·50	19·5	22	130	473	98
Good	70	12	7½	490	22·25	19·6	22	129	455	99
	65	11½	7	471	21·75	19·7	21	126	449	101
	60	11½	6½	451	21·50	19·9	21	124	441	102
Average	55	11	6	431	21·00	20·0	21	121	437	103
	50	10½	5½	417	20·50	20·1	20	120	428	104
	45	9½	5½	363	20·25	20·2	20	119	421	105
Fair	40	9	5	348	19·75	20·3	20	116	414	106
	35	8½	4½	330	19·50	20·4	19	115	404	107
	30	7½	4	287	19·25	20·5	19	114	395	108
Poor	25	6½	3	226	18·75	20·7	18	108	386	109
	20	5½	2	204	18·50	21·0	17	101	378	109
	15	5	2	183	17·75	21·2	15	97	365	111
Very Poor	10	3½	1½	163	17·25	21·5	13	94	347	112
	5	2½	0	75	16·00	22·0	7	87	334	115
	0	1	0	37	13·00	22·0	5	85	320	124
Range =	0 and 100th Percentile Scores									
Mean =		9·924	5·734	391·5	20·71	20·07	19·36	118·7	430·0	103·6
Standard Devn. =		4·68	3·435	192·0	3·065	0·85	4·875	17·32	60·24	6·91
No. of subjects =		46	77	46	77	77	77	77	77	77
Mean Age =	16–22 years (SD = 0·5309)									

Mean Weight = 166·8 lb. (SD = 20·35) Mean Height = 70·25 ins. (SD = 2·633)

[1] Rogers' SI
[2] Rogers' SI
[3] Rogers' Index $\left[\text{Pull Up} + \text{Push Up}\right]\left[\dfrac{Wt(lb.)}{10} + Ht(in.) - 60\right]$
[4] Jump and Reach (Morgan and Adamson)
[5] Fleishman (5 × 20 yards)
[6] Fleishman (in 30 secs.)
[7] Dominant Hand (Loughborough)
   Triple-Thrust Grip Dynamometer
[8] Rank Dynamometer (Salter Scale)
[9] Circular Track (Grass and Cinder)

TABLE III
Physical Fitness Profile Record of Welsh Youth Rugby Players—Backs: 15-17 years

Classification	Percentile score	Bar[1] dips	Pull[2] up	Arm[3] strength	Vertical[4] jump	Shuttle[5] run	Leg[6] lifts	Grip[7] strength	Back[8] lift	600 yards[9] run
		No.	No.	Score	In.	Secs.	No.	lb.	lb.	Secs.
Excellent	100	28	12	824	28·00	18·0	28	150	485	88
	95	20½	11½	691	26·25	18·1	25	136	467	90
	90	18	11	637	25·00	18·3	23	131	450	93
Very Good	85	17	10	600	24·25	18·6	23	126	439	94
	80	16½	9½	582	23·50	18·7	22	121	431	95
	75	16	9	572	23·25	18·8	22	120	421	96
Good	70	15½	8½	561	23·00	18·9	22	116	411	97
	65	14½	8½	542	22·75	19·0	21	113	401	97
	60	14	8	521	22·50	19·1	21	110	338	98
Average	55	13½	8	496	22·00	19·2	21	108	380	98
	50	13	7½	461	21·75	19·3	20	105	374	99
	45	12½	7½	423	21·25	19·4	90	105	366	100
Fair	40	12	7	417	20·75	19·6	20	104	361	101
	35	11½	7	400	20·25	19·7	20	100	356	102
	30	11	6	387	20·00	19·9	19	99	352	102
Poor	25	10	6	369	19·50	20·0	19	96	347	105
	20	9½	6	357	18·50	20·2	18	93	335	105
	15	8½	5½	338	18·00	20·3	17	90	321	107
Very Poor	10	7½	5	323	17·75	20·5	17	88	312	109
	5	5½	4	241	16·25	21·0	15	80	300	112
	0	4	3	140	15·00	21·0	14	70	265	116
Range	0 and 100th Percentile Scores									
Mean		13·8	7·63	469·5	21·25	19·31	20·21	107·6	379·3	100·2
Standard Devn.		4·51	2·2	137·8	2·835	0·762	2·79	16·33	51·3	6·25
No. of subjects		52	72	52	72	72	72	72	72	71
Mean Age		16·25 years (SD = 0·481)	Mean Weight = 144·1 lb. (SD = 14·11)					Mean Height = 68·29 in. (SD = 2·15)		

1 Rogers' SI
2 Rogers' SI
3 Rogers' Index [Pull Up + Push Up] $\left[\frac{\text{Wt (lb.)}}{10} + \text{Ht (in.)} - 60\right]$
4 Jump and Reach (Morgan and Adamson)
5 Fleishman (5 × 20 yards)
6 Fleishman (in 30 secs.)
7 Dominant Hand (Loughborough Triple-Thrust Grip Dynamometer)
8 Rank Dynamometer (Salter Scale)
9 Circular Track (Grass and Cinder)

TABLE IV

Physical Fitness Profile Record of Welsh Youth Rugby Players—Forwards: 17–19 years

Classification	Percentile score	Bar[1] dips	Pull[2] up	Arm[3] strength	Vertical[4] jump	Shuttle[5] run	Leg[6] lifts	Grip[7] strength	Back[8] lift	600 yard[9] run
		No.	No.	Score	In.	Secs.	No.	lb.	lb.	Secs.
Excellent	100	37	16	1373	32·00	18·0	29	150	620	89
	95	22	10½	890	26·00	18·5	27	150	558	91
	90	20½	9½	780	25·00	18·7	25	143	538	93
Very Good	85	18½	8½	741	24·25	18·8	24	139	523	94
	80	17½	8	701	24·00	19·0	24	135	507	95
	75	16½	7½	640	23·75	19·1	23	131	498	96
Good	70	16	7	606	23·25	19·2	23	129	483	97
	65	15½	6½	581	23·00	19·4	22	126	478	97
	60	14½	6½	570	22·75	19·5	22	125	470	98
Average	55	13½	6	545	22·25	19·6	21	122	464	99
	50	13	5½	508	21·75	19·7	21	120	456	100
	45	12	5½	495	21·50	19·9	21	120	449	101
Fair	40	11	5	480	21·00	20·0	20	118	440	102
	35	10½	4½	449	20·75	20·1	20	115	432	102
	30	10	4½	417	20·50	20·2	19	113	428	103
Poor	25	9	4	362	20·00	20·4	19	111	419	104
	20	8	3½	322	19·50	20·5	18	109	406	105
	15	6	2½	295	19·25	20·8	17	105	399	107
Very Poor	10	5	2	232	18·75	21·1	16	103	381	109
	5	3½	1	152	18·00	21·4	14	100	372	111
	0	1	0	30	16·00	22·0	13	80	310	120

0 and 100th Percentile Scores

		Bar[1] dips	Pull[2] up	Arm[3] strength	Vertical[4] jump	Shuttle[5] run	Leg[6] lifts	Grip[7] strength	Back[8] lift	600 yard[9] run
Range	=			516·7	21·77	19·76	20·82	121·7	458·1	100·4
Mean	=	12·88	5·68	222·7	2·56	0·802	3·70	15·43	63·33	6·01
Standard Devn.	=	5·86	2·93	145	194	194	194	194	119	194
No. of subjects	=	145	194							
Mean Age	=	18·06 years (SD = 0·7363)								

Mean Weight = 177·3 lb. (SD = 20·06)

Mean Height = 70·90 in. (SD = 2·331)

[1] Rogers' SI
[2] Rogers' SI
[3] Rogers' Index [Pull Up + Push Up] $\left[\dfrac{\text{Wt (lb.)}}{10} + \text{Ht (in.)} - 60 \right]$
[4] Jump and Reach (Morgan and Adamson)
[5] Fleishman (5 × 20 yards)
[6] Fleishman (in 30 secs.)
[7] Dominant Hand (Loughborough Triple-Thrust Grip Dynamometer)
[8] Rank Dynamometer (Salter Scale)
[9] Circular Track (Grass and Cinder)

TABLE V
Physical Fitness Profile Record of Welsh Youth Rugby Players—Backs: 17–19 years

Classification	Percentile score	Bar[1] dips	Pull[2] up	Arm[3] strength	Vertical[4] jump	Shuttle[5] run	Leg[6] lifts	Grip[7] strength	Back[8] lift	600 yard[9] run
		No.	*No.*	*Score*	*In.*	*Secs.*	*No.*	*lb.*	*lb.*	*Secs.*
Excellent	100	37	19	1029	30·00	17·3	28	150	575	83
	95	25	10	871	27·00	17·7	27	141	503	88
	90	23	9½	785	26·00	17·8	25	130	471	90
Very Good	85	20½	9	729	25·50	18·0	24	129	459	91
	80	20	8½	698	25·00	18·2	24	126	454	92
	75	19	8	672	24·50	18·4	24	120	448	94
Good	70	18½	8	650	23·75	18·5	23	119	441	94
	65	18	7½	637	23·50	18·7	23	116	438	94
	60	17½	7	620	23·00	18·8	22	115	428	95
Average	55	17	7	609	22·75	18·9	22	113	418	96
	50	16½	6½	591	22·50	19·0	22	110	414	97
	45	16	6	564	22·00	19·1	21	110	410	98
Fair	40	15½	6	546	21·50	19·2	21	106	404	99
	35	15	5½	528	21·25	19·3	20	105	397	99
	30	14½	5	510	20·75	19·4	20	104	389	100
Poor	25	13½	4	497	20·25	19·6	20	101	383	101
	20	13	4	474	19·75	19·8	19	100	372	103
	15	12½	3½	451	19·25	20·0	19	98	361	105
Very Poor	10	11½	3	403	18·75	20·2	18	94	349	108
	5	10½	2	364	18·00	20·4	17	89	324	110
	0	5	2	225	14·00	21·8	10	80	276	116

0 and 100th Percentile Scores

		Bar	Pull	Arm	Vertical	Shuttle	Leg	Grip	Back	600 yard
Range	=	132	148	132	148	148	148	148	127	148
Mean	=	16·84	7·956	591·2	22·19	18·99	21·57	112·0	414·2	97·67
Standard Devn.	=	4·60	2·56	147·8	2·76	0·773	3·15	14·76	53·01	6·73
No. of subjects	=	132	148	132	148	148	148	148	127	148
Mean Age	=	18·03 years (SD = 0·719)								

Mean Weight = 153·5 lb. (SD = 14·04)

Mean Height = 68·59 in. (SD = 2·097)

[1] Rogers' SI

[2] Rogers' SI

[3] Rogers' Index |Pull Up + Push Up| $\left[\dfrac{Wt\ (lb.)}{10} + Ht\ (in.) - 60\right]$

[4] Jump and Reach (Morgan and Adamson)

[5] Fleishman (5 × 20 yards)

[6] Fleishman (in 30 secs.)

[7] Dominant Hand (Loughborough Triple Thrust Grip Dynamometer)

[8] Rank Dynamometer (Salter Scale)

[9] Circular Track (Grass and Cinder)

BIBLIOGRAPHY
The references below are given for the benefit of those who wish to delve deeper in the fitness field:

1. ADAMSON, G. T. "Training Methods", *Journal of Chartered Soc. of Physiotherapy*, June 1972.
2. COUPON, H. Personal communications with E. Gwyn Evans, 1975.
3. EVANS, E. G. "Training for Strength and Power", Address given at WRU Coaching Conference, November 1973.
4. EVANS, E. G. "Fitness Scores of Welsh Youth Rugby Players", *Brit. Journal of Sports Medicine*, December 1968.
5. EVANS, E. G. "Basic Fitness Testing of Rugby Football Players", *BJSM*, December 1973.
6. FAULKNER, J. A. "New Perspectives in Training for Maximum Performances", *JAMA*, 9th September 1968.
7. GIBSON, A. J. "A Review of some factors affecting Sprint Speed", *Athletics Coach*, March 1976.
8. HOCKEY, R. V. *Physical Fitness*, Mosby, 1973.
9. HOLT, J. B. Translation of "L'Amicale des Entraîneurs Français d'Athlétisme No. 90", *Athletics Coach*, March 1976.
10. HOWELL, M. L. and MARFORD, W. R. *Fitness Training Methods*, CAHPER, 1970.
11. JENSEN, C. R. and FISHER, A. G. *Scientific Basis of Athletic Conditioning*, Lea and Febiger, Philadelphia, 1972.
12. WILLIAMS, C., COUTTS and REID "Observations on the aerobic power of university Rugby players and professional soccer players", *BJSM*, December 1973.

SECTION IV
Quo Vadis?

How nice it would be if we knew precisely where we were going. It is usually popular to do a little crystal-ball gazing and in this, the last part of my book, I am going to be no exception. Before I do, however, perhaps I should make it clear that these are my own personal views and are not necessarily those held by the Welsh Rugby Union.

Early on in my book I wrote about participation, competition and coaching as being key factors in raising standards. I have, no doubt, presented enough views on coaching, but I think the other two are worthy of mention too.

PARTICIPATION

"The more milk you have, the more cream you get", or, "The broader the base the higher the apex". These are popular statements in relation to many aspects of community life, and they are Rugby truisms provided they are related to the other previously mentioned factors. It is not too difficult to have mass participation at low level with a very small apex. I would be the last to suggest that everybody who plays Rugby should be totally dedicated and train seven times a week. I recognise the worth of G. K. Chesterton's statement, "If a thing's worth doing, then it's worth doing badly". Rugby football, with its unique social atmosphere, can give great pleasure and enjoyment to hundreds of young men whose playing standards are light years away from those displayed at the Cardiff Arms Park, Eden Park, Ellis Park and Twickenham. These people, however, are just as essential to the game as the most famous internationals.

Fortunately it is not an either/or choice: the game can, and should, cater for everyone, the ambitious and the unambitious. In fact most Rugby Unions should have such aims written into their constitution. Among the Objects of the Welsh Rugby Union is one which states, "To promote, foster, encourage and improve the standard of play of Amateur Rugby Union Football in Wales". It can be seen immediately that this is all embracing. "To promote", is essentially to get more people taking part, and in a society where there are many activities competing for the time and interest of young men it is important that every effort should be made to sell Rugby football as a game or, even better, as a way of life. My Union is very keenly aware of its responsibilities in this respect, and is widely admired for the way it has supported school and youth Rugby in Wales. We have gone even further than this in trying to help the emerging Rugby countries. Many Rugby men from abroad have been invited to Wales on short tours: Fiji, Canada, Tonga, Japan, Argentina are examples. Welsh coaches and referees are in demand throughout the Rugby world and the Welsh Rugby Union Committee are ever ready to send aid of this kind. In fact the Four Home Unions have a great record in this field and British coaches and referees are spreading Rugby expertise far and wide.

"To improve", means creating the opportunity for every player to develop to his full potential, and in outlining the structure and organisation of Welsh Rugby I was able to illustrate quite clearly how talent can be spotted and then followed through to senior level. In this way the game becomes self-generating because success breeds interest and interest in turn, properly channelled, can breed success.

COMPETITION

Perhaps the term "Competition" is the most misunderstood in the Rugby vocabulary. Mention it to some people and they throw up their hands in horror. They react as though there is something unsavoury about it. It is something to do with winning cups and medals and that is not quite nice! Of course competition can be abused; of course it can lead to an over-serious approach; of course it can produce a poor quality of game; but it does not have to do any of these things. Anyway, what is the alternative, non-competitive Rugby?

Every game is a competition and Rugby football through the world is full of competitive Rugby structures, some based on leagues, others on a knock-out system. The trouble is that in many countries, as in Wales, the competition is fragmented and the game does not benefit to the extent I believe it would if the competitions were nationally organised. Organised competition coupled with a progressive coaching scheme would, in my view, have a definite influence in raising standards. This is not to say that it cannot raise problems too, but that is where the challenge lies.

Apart from raising standards one has to take into account the interest which competition produces, and interest expresses itself in the form of finance and the motivation of young players who wish to take part in the game. Both finance and motivation are crucial to the continued prosperity and development of the game.

The Welsh Rugby Union Challenge Cup is a case in point. In the 1976 Cup Final, the attendance was in excess of 32,000 and the gate receipts £33,000. In Scotland since the introduction of the Scottish Leagues there have been greatly increased attendances at all games. In the 1975 Scotland v. Wales match at Murrayfield there was a world record Rugby crowd: 104,000 was the official attendance but it is known that there were thousands more inside the ground and many thousands more outside. Scotland won 12–10!

It is my opinion that leagues, in terms of standards, would be more beneficial than knock-out competitions, because players and teams at all levels could match their skills in a competitive atmosphere on a regular basis. In my ideal set-up I would have both kinds of competition.

Wales probably has the most intensive club Rugby system in

the world, but it does not have the impact it would have if it were based on a national competition. The Welsh Rugby Union Committee have explored the possibility of establishing national leagues on a promotion and relegation basis which would allow deserving clubs to improve their fixture lists. Unfortunately, although there was overwhelming support for the idea from the majority of clubs, those clubs whose presence is essential if the scheme is to be viable have declined to participate. This, of course, in an amateur game is their democratic right, but these are early days yet and some time in the future there may be a change of heart.

PRESSURE ON PLAYERS

There is no doubt that the present-day first-class player in Wales and perhaps to a lesser extent in Britain is under tremendous pressure. The demands of the game have increased—higher levels of fitness which means more time; attendance at club coaching sessions, more time; selection for representative squads, more time; an increase in short terms during the close season, more time. All these demands lead me to believe that we are asking for a commitment from amateur Rugby players which is greater than that expected from professional soccer players. The Rugby man is trying to do it all in his spare time. Somewhere along the line he has to earn a living. It is a worrying situation and it could be the greatest threat to the amateur status of the game.

Fortunately, at least in Wales, clubs now have tended to curb enthusiastic Treasurers whose sole object seemed to be to persuade the Fixture Secretary to arrange fixtures on any free day. This, coupled with the advent of floodlights, meant that clubs were playing two and sometimes three games in one week. In a contact game like Rugby this is an impossible task. There does, however, seem to be some rationalisation and an attempt has been made to ease back on fixtures.

This situation does not occur in most overseas countries. In

New Zealand, for instance, it is rare for the average club player to play in excess of 20 matches in a season, even an All Black will only manage about 30. Welsh players often play twice as many, and I do know of one player who reputedly played over 100 games in one season! The whole matter needs to be kept continually under review, otherwise there could be an unfortunate backlash.

LAWS

I have never been one who wished to rewrite the Law Book every season as some people apparently do. It would be a pointless exercise. The International Rugby Football Board, who are the Law makers, quite rightly resist too many changes in the Laws. It is surprising how long it takes for a new Law to be understood and accepted by players. It may mean the relearning of technique or developing a totally new skill and this does not happen overnight.

On the other hand there does seem to be a strong argument for the alteration or even removal of some Laws. I personally can find little justification for the retention of the fair catch. It causes a great deal of controversy over decisions, and I think the game would be better without it. I would even be prepared to accept a modification because I find it totally unacceptable that, because a player catches the ball, something he is expected to do anyway, and assuming he is standing still and calls "mark" he is then given a free kick, which, if he is near enough to goal, can be turned into three points.

In the same kind of category is the drop-out which takes place after the defending side has touched-down the ball. They have an immediate gain of 22 metres and I fail to see the justice in this.

My friends from Australia have campaigned for some time to ban a scrum half from crossing the centre line through the tunnel in pursuit of his opposite number. They want the scrum half of the side in possession to be able to move the ball away without any threat of interference. I cannot accept this view for it will make the scrum half's job too easy. I am convinced that the reason they have advocated this change is because the majority of Australian hookers hook with the near foot. This tends to produce a lot of bad ball and consequently puts more pressure on the scrum half. The real answer to their problem is to seek quality possession at the scrum, and they should begin by getting hookers to use the far foot. In fairness many of their hookers are beginning to change, and it will be interesting to see if the Australian Rugby Union persist in their attempts to modify the Law and prevent scrum halves from chasing their opposite numbers.

I suppose, however, that the most controversial issues concerning Laws is that of the differential penalty. My old friends Vivian Jenkins of the *Sunday Times* and J. B. G. Thomas of the *Western Mail* have fought a long campaign on this topic. One could say that progress is being made because the IRFB have now agreed to look at the matter and are collecting statistical evidence as well as suggestions as to how such a Law may be implemented. It is not really a simple matter. There are those who argue that the way to reduce penalty goals is not to eliminate the penalty offence but to increase the points for a penalty goal. Others say that the removal of a penalty kick for a technical offence would remove the deterrent and there would be an increase in technical offences. There is an answer to this one and that is that referees would have to interpret persistent infringement more strictly.

I do not think that there is much doubt that the majority of people would like to see some differentiation in the penalty for foul play, misconduct and obstruction, as opposed to the technical offences such as off-side and "foot-up" in the scrum. Arguments have been advanced that the penalty play for foul play should be a penalty kick from in front of the goal posts, irrespective of where the offence took place. This is not a practical solution: suppose one player committed such an offence on his opposition's goal-line. The game would stop and there would be a trek to the other end of the field for the kick to be taken. It would destroy any fluency there happened to be in the game.

One solution might be to allow a direct kick at goal for any foul-play offence and an indirect kick for technical offences, with the proviso that either kind of offence in the 22-metre area would result in a direct kick at goal. It might minimise the tendency for an increase in technical offences. I think that there will be an attempt very soon to resolve the kicking dilemma and I know that Vivian Jenkins and J. B. G. Thomas will be highly delighted.

REFEREES

I must confess that there is one aspect of refereeing where I think we are in danger of losing our way. I am referring specifically to the advantage law and the way it is being applied. Referees are urged to play the advantage law to the limit and to let the game run. I am beginning to think that perhaps we have gone too far in this direction, and the result is a casual and loose approach by the referee which produces loose play. Players for the most part appreciate the referee who is strict—that does not mean that he cannot play advantage, but many referees become so obsessed by advantage that, in effect, they fail to referee the game.

I often think, too, that referees fail to appreciate what constitutes advantage. Part of Law 8 on advantage states, "The referee shall not whistle for an infringement which is followed by an advantage gained by the non-offending team. An advantage must be either territorial or such possession of the ball as constitutes an obvious tactical advantage. A mere opportunity to gain advantage is not sufficient."

It is the last sentence which is most significant because in my opinion more and more referees are waiting longer and longer to see if an advantage will accrue. I have on occasions seen play move 30 yards only for the referee to whistle and bring it back. That is not how advantage should be played.

Furthermore, once a referee has allowed advantage—and he

must decide this fairly quickly—he should then allow play to continue and, if the side that has been given the advantage, mess it up by their own incompetence, the referee should not whistle and bring play back to the point where he allowed advantage.

I recently watched one of Britain's most distinguished referees officiate in a representative game. There was a scrum in front of the goal posts and the attacking side won possession. The referee, although the defenders offended, allowed the advantage. Play continued until the attacking team just failed to score in the corner. The referee then brought them back and gave a penalty kick under the posts. I discussed it with him afterwards and he agreed that he had been wrong. He admitted that he had given the attacking team "a second bite at the cherry". It is an area of refereeing which requires some serious rethinking.

RUGBY INJURIES

Recently Rugby has come under considerable fire via the media concerning injuries which occur during the game. Some of the comment has been unjust because it has not presented the complete picture. Rugby authorities have been accused of being insensitive to the welfare of their players, of neglecting their responsibilities and of taking part in a "conspiracy of silence" when any serious injury occurs which may be the result of foul play. Obviously I cannot speak for all Rugby authorities, but I can state what the Welsh Rugby Union's attitude is in such matters and my information is that at least the other Home Unions are equally responsible.

One cannot escape from the fact that Rugby football is a physical contact game. Indeed this is one of its appeals. Unfortunately such a game often produces trauma, whether it be a result of player contact with the ground or player with player. The incidence of injury is not very high and statistically severe injuries are rare. Our view is that even one player seriously injured is one player too many and therefore we have to take whatever steps are necessary to protect players from any kind of injury as far as is possible.

We therefore have the WRU's medical consultants lecturing on Rugby injuries at our coaches' conference. They speak in particular about the prevention of injury. Many are avoidable. The correct equipment, boots, padded goal posts, flexible corner posts, anti-tetanus injections, shin pad, mouth guards etc. can often dramatically reduce the number of injuries. Correct technique in relation to tackling, scrummaging, rucking and mauling can help, so can higher standards of fitness. Scrum collapses have recently caused a number of very severe injuries and in some cases it is known that the scrum collapse was a deliberate act. Medical men can describe in graphic terms the likely results of such foolish and dangerous practices and this cannot fail to impress coaches and players.

Time too is spent at such conferences on the treatment of injuries. Coaches are told emphatically that any player who loses consciousness on the field, even momentarily, should be removed for a doctor's opinion. The dangers of the use of pain-killing injections are also pointed out. Every attempt is made to make coaches as well informed as possible.

The Welsh Rugby Union as long ago as 1968 organised a course for club trainers. It was exceptionally well attended and most worthwhile. We are now considering ways in which we can further help those who deal with first-aid on the field.

All courses for players have, on the staff, a man who is totally responsible for the medical side. If it is first-aid that is required, then he gives it. If it is medical treatment, then he sees that the player is taken to the appropriate place. In the same way at National Squad sessions the Union's medical consultants and physiotherapist are in attendance to deal with any problems that may arise. All these facts surely indicate that we are concerned for the welfare of our players.

Furthermore, foul play is severely punished, and this is a further indication of our determination to protect players from undisciplined acts.

Mention too ought to be made of the Irish Rugby Football

Union's immense contribution in this area. As part of their centenary celebrations in 1975 they arranged a medical congress on injuries in Rugby football and other sports. It was well attended and addressed by distinguished doctors and sportsmen.

THE OVERSEAS CHALLENGE

I suppose in some respects I have more overseas coaching experience than perhaps any other person. As long ago as 1965 I went to Canada and the USA. In 1967 I spent three weeks in Ceylon. In 1970 as a Churchill Fellow I had the unique experience of going to Ceylon, Australia, New Zealand, Fiji and British Columbia, a tour that lasted two months. Since that time, I have been to Australia (for a second time), the Bahamas, Spain and Italy, as well as meeting a great number of overseas coaches who attend Welsh Rugby Union courses as observers. I feel therefore that I am well qualified to comment on the world scene.

One of my outstanding memories was representing the WRU at the RFU's Centenary Congress in 1970. Imaginative in its conception and superb in its organisation, it demonstrated that Rugby football covered the world. Fifty countries were represented on that occasion, ranging from the biggest of the world's Rugby nations to the smallest with only a few clubs. They were, however, equal in one thing and that was enthusiasm and love for the game. While it is true to say that the game in most of the overseas countries was initially started by British expatriates, the indigenous people are now very much in evidence both in administration and playing. For instance, some years ago a Canadian National XV would have been composed of a large number of British players. The situation is now reversed, the majority of players would be Canadian born.

However, all these countries look to the International Rugby Football Board and in particular, to the Four Home Unions for help and guidance. They continually ask for assistance in coaching, refereeing, publications, films etc. Probably, however, the most potent aid comes in the form of club tours to and from Great Britain. At the beginning and the end of each season, Great Britain is usually host to a large number of club teams from all over the world—Argentinians, Americans, Australians, Belgians, Dutch, French, Italians, New Zealanders, Spaniards all gravitate towards the Four Home Union Countries, and now reciprocal club visits are being arranged. This is a marvellous way to raise standards.

It is significant, too, how the lead given by Wales in the organisation of coaching has been taken up by other countries. When the RFU *Guide to Coaches* was written, part of our argument (in Pamphlet No. 1 concerned with Philosophy and Attitude) was based on what took place in New Zealand and South Africa. We argued that if we were to raise our standards then we had to develop a coaching structure which was at least the equal of that in those two great Rugby countries. Ironically, later I realised that our views were based on a false premise.

When the Springboks came to Britain in 1969, Avril Malan, the Springbok Coach and former captain, urgently sought discussions with me to find out what we were doing. I learnt then that there was no coaching scheme in South Africa and in Malan's view there was very little coaching either. I remember, too, talking to Danie Craven and his saying to me that Wales were at that time three years ahead of South Africa. This was widely reported in the press and, eventually, Danie Craven explained that what he meant was that Wales were three years ahead of South Africa in the appointment of a Coaching Organiser—we are now nine years ahead!

It is interesting to note, however, that four provinces in South Africa have now got full-time men whose responsibility is to develop the game through coaching. One of them, Roger Gardner, comes from Wales and is a WRU Coach. As far as I ascertain there is still no move to make a national appointment in South Africa. I would have thought that this was crucial. As it is, at least four provincial unions will be developing their own schemes and playing patterns and this will make it increasing difficulty to weld a South African team into a cohesive unit—apart from the problems caused by differing standards relating to the assessment of coaches. South Africa of course have other difficulties, they are political, and it would not be appropriate for me to comment upon them in a book of this nature.

I spent one month in New Zealand in 1970. Now there is a Rugby Country. Once again, however, I was surprised. I found that there was no coaching scheme at all. They had a system, and that was that each XV in a club, and some clubs have more than 30 teams, had a coach. He had no training and relatively little help. When a player hung up his boots, if he was interested, he went into coaching and started in the lower XVs and gradually worked his way to the higher grades. Some provincial unions organised short courses for coaches, but in our terms they would be relatively unsophisticated.

I have always felt that All Black teams have accepted too low a standard, they have settled for winning. With all their magnificent physical material, their expertise and their enthusiasm, the type of game which they could play has no horizons; but I think that they did not see the need to try to develop their game. "After all," one man said to me, "we are the best in the world." I said to him, "Yes, you are, at the moment, but don't you want to get any better?" There is no doubt that defeat in South Africa in 1970 was a great shock for New Zealand Rugby, but to lose the series to the Lions in 1971 was, in New Zealand's eyes, a disaster.

At last they began to rethink their game. They looked at their coaching structure. National courses for young players have been developed with John J. Stewart as Director. They still have not made any full-time coaching appointment, a position which is vital for the development of any coaching scheme, but I understand that certain rumblings are taking place.

Australia, on the other hand, with much less in terms of resources, realised the need to up-date their game. The Australian

Rugby Union approached the WRU early in 1974 to see whether I could be released to go to Australia and advise them on the establishment of a coaching scheme. They also took another significant step, and that was the appointment of a National Coaching Director. It was no coincidence that on the very day I landed in Australia, on 1st April 1974, Dick Marks, their Coaching Director, started work. We travelled throughout Australia and Dick already has done a tremendous job for Australian Rugby.

Several other countries have also made similar appointments. They are not yet great countries in the Rugby sense but the efforts they are making will certainly repay great dividends. Canada has a Coaching Director, Don Burgess, and the Canadian provincial unions are also working to this end. In fact, Ontario Rugby Union have appointed Larry Nancekvill as their Coaching Director. Larry came to Aberystwyth on the WRU Coaches Course some years ago. Both he and Don Burgess have been to Britain, seeking help and guidance.

Italy is perhaps the most interesting case. Their Technical Adviser is Roy Bish, a former WRU Staff Coach and Coach to Cardiff Rugby Club. He is a man with vast experience and he is doing a first-class job for the Italian Rugby Federation. The results Italy have achieved in matches against other FIRA countries since Roy's appointment are most impressive. Italy could well be going places in Rugby terms.

Holland also have a British coach as their Coaching Adviser. He is Dennis Power formerly of Bristol and he, too, is working very hard to raise standards.

France, of course, is the country which dominates FIRA. They have a foot in both camps—in the International Board, although they are not members, and FIRA. French Rugby is admired and respected. They have tremendous resources, both in terms of finance and playing strength. I was told recently that there are over 1,000 French clubs running "Schools of Rugby" for young players on Wednesday afternoons. In some cases as many as 250 boys take part in one "School". It is a frightening thought. Through the Ministry of Sport each province has a full-time Rugby Adviser and there are about 18 working at the moment. France have never been able to develop the National Squad concept, but they have a number of national teams below senior level, such as school, youth, Under-21 and "B" XV. Their "B" XV for instance, plays about nine matches in a season, and this is obviously good preparation for players for the senior National XV.

A remarkable standard of Rugby in relation to their size has been achieved by Fiji and Tonga. Wales brought Fiji to the Principality in 1964 and everyone was absolutely delighted with their attitude, skill and total dedication to running Rugby. It was a memorable tour and culminated in a most exciting game against a Welsh XV on the Cardiff Arms Park. Fiji came again in 1970 as part of the RFU Centenary celebrations, but the Rugby did not reach the élan of their first tour. There were reasons. In the first place, in 1964 we were suffering from a surfeit of negative Rugby and any attempt to run the ball was welcomed with open arms. By 1970 British Rugby's ball-winning capacity had been much improved and Fiji found themselves in the same position that British sides facing Springboks and All Blacks used to be in; they could not get the ball.

Tonga also came to Wales, and they too found winning the ball their greatest problem. Both Fiji and Tonga have splendid physical material but they lack sophisticated ball-winning techniques. Therefore they cannot win enough ball to demonstrate their tremendous running, handling and support skills. If they wish to compete on equal terms they will have, in the future, to pay more attention to ball-winning. I think that they can achieve this without losing any of the great flair they undoubtedly have for playing Rugby football.

In complete contrast is Japan. They have a most sophisticated approach to the game but because of their size, they are often at a grave disadvantage. However, they think deeply about the game;

they are one of the largest Rugby playing countries in the world and consequently they have a large reservoir of players. They have a good deal to offer Rugby, because of the thought which they have given to trying to overcome the size disadvantage. We can certainly learn from them.

The United States of America RFU has recently been formed, although Rugby has been played there for a long time. The USA is probably the biggest Rugby-growth area in the world. One hears awesome stories of the size and speed of some of their players, and there is no doubt that properly harnessed, America could become a potent Rugby force. But I happen to believe that it will take a lot longer than many people think. While they may have a lot of players with terrific potential, the facilities are not good and finance is a problem. Most adult sport in the States is professional and their society is geared to professional sport. This alone is going to make it most difficult for an amateur game like Rugby to develop. There is no government aid for sport in the States so finance is bound to be a problem. However, there is much enthusiasm and in 10 to 20 years the position could look a lot more promising.

EPILOGUE

I can think of no better way of ending than by quoting from my book *Rugby for Beginners*.

We have read a lot about principles of play, techniques, skills and means of developing them but, expert though we may be at these things, if our personal attitudes towards the game are wrong then our success will only be temporary.

Rugby football has survived for well over a hundred years and become one of the World's greatest amateur sports as much by the spirit it creates as by the skill with which it is played. In this modern age it is often "clever" to sneer at terms like the "spirit of the game" and "ethics", but Rugby football, in company with other sports, has demonstrated on many occasions that these qualities are not entirely lost. Of course there have been instances when the halo has slipped temporarily but these have only emphasised what a precious heritage we possess. It is our responsibility, those of us who play and coach the game, to preserve and enrich it. We must ensure by our actions, both on and off the field, that we do nothing to discredit the game.

One of the features of Rugby football is that it is a game of physical contact and it is inevitable that hard knocks will be given and taken. It is vital that these take place within the context of the game. Any player taking part in this kind of physical contest knows that there is an injury risk even though the ethics and the laws may be strictly observed. He should never be subjected to risks which are outside both ethics and law.

In essence we must respect the game and those who take part in it. We must especially respect the authority of the referee.

His judgement and decision must be final, accepted without hesitation and certainly without question.

Presumably we play the game because we enjoy it, that is probably the best reason. But let us remember that there is no disgrace in wanting to be successful; there is no dishonour in wanting to win. All players should pursue excellence, each, according to his ability, will achieve varying degrees of success. We cannot all be internationals but we can all display high standards of behaviour and sportsmanship. Defeat must be accepted with good grace and victory with humility.

Perhaps, however, all I am trying to say can be summed up so much better, and in far fewer words, by quoting from the Object of the Game which is part of the Laws of Rugby Union Football. It says the Object of the Game is that two teams "observing fair play according to the Laws and a sporting spirit, should by carrying, passing and kicking the ball, score as many points as possible, the team scoring the greater number of points to be the winner of the match".

GOOD LUCK and GOOD RUGBY